Teacher's Handbook

Lawrence Lawson

OXFORD
UNIVERSITY PRESS

UNIVERSITY PRESS

198 Madison Avenue
New York, NY 10016 USA

Great Clarendon Street, Oxford OX2 6DP UK

Oxford University Press is a department of the University of Oxford.
It furthers the University's objective of excellence in research, scholarship,
and education by publishing worldwide in

Oxford New York

Auckland Cape Town Dar es Salaam Hong Kong Karachi
Kuala Lumpur Madrid Melbourne Mexico City Nairobi
New Delhi Shanghai Taipei Toronto

With offices in

Argentina Austria Brazil Chile Czech Republic France Greece
Guatemala Hungary Italy Japan Poland Portugal Singapore
South Korea Switzerland Thailand Turkey Ukraine Vietnam

OXFORD and OXFORD ENGLISH are registered trademarks of
Oxford University Press.

General Manager, American ELT: Laura Pearson
Publisher: Stephanie Karras
Associate Publishing Manager: Sharon Sargent
Associate Development Editor: Keyana Shaw
Director, ADP: Susan Sanguily
Executive Design Manager: Maj-Britt Hagsted
Associate Design Manager: Michael Steinhofer
Electronic Production Manager: Julie Armstrong
Production Artist: Elissa Santos
Cover Design: Michael Steinhofer
Production Coordinator: Elizabeth Matsumoto

ISBN: 978-0-19-475618-1 Listening and Speaking 4 Teacher's Handbook Pack
ISBN: 978-0-19-475661-7 Listening and Speaking 4 Teacher's Handbook
ISBN: 978-0-19-475665-5 Listening and Speaking 4/Reading and Writing 4
                    Testing Program CD-ROM
ISBN: 978-0-19-475643-3 Q Online Practice Teacher Access Code Card

Printed in China

This book is printed on paper from certified and well-managed sources.

10 9 8 7 6 5 4 3

ACKNOWLEDGMENTS

*The publishers would like to thank the following for their kind permission to reproduce
photographs:*

p. vi Marcin Krygier/iStockphoto; xiii Rüstem GÜRLER/iStockphoto

CONTENTS

WELCOME TO Q:Skills for Success

Q: Skills for Success is a six-level series with two strands,
Reading and Writing and *Listening and Speaking*.

WITH Q ONLINE PRACTICE

STUDENT AND TEACHER INFORMED

Q: Skills for Success is the result of an extensive development process involving thousands of teachers and hundreds of students around the world. Their views and opinions helped shape the content of the series. *Q* is grounded in teaching theory as well as real-world classroom practice, making it the most learner-centered series available.

To the Teacher

Highlights of the *Q: Skills for Success* Teacher's Handbook

As you probably know from your own teaching experience, students want to know the point of a lesson. They want to know the "why" even when they understand the "how." In the classroom, the "why" is the learning outcome, and to be successful, students need to know it. The learning outcome provides a clear reason for classroom work and helps students meaningfully access new material.

Each unit in Oxford's *Q: Skills for Success* series builds around a thought-provoking question related to that unit's unique learning outcome. Students learn vocabulary to answer the unit question; consider new information related to the unit's theme that utilizes this vocabulary; use this information to think critically about new questions; and use those answers to practice the new listening, vocabulary, grammar, pronunciation, and speaking skills they need to achieve the unit's learning outcome.

Each aspect of the learning process in the Q series builds toward completing the learning outcome. This interconnected process of considering new information is at the heart of a critical thinking approach and forms the basis of the students' work in each unit of the Q series. At the end of the unit, students complete a practical project built around the learning outcome.

Learning outcomes create expectations in the classroom: expectations of what students will learn, what teachers will teach, and what lessons will focus on. Students benefit because they know they need to learn content for a purpose; teachers benefit because they can plan activities that reinforce the knowledge and skills students need to complete the learning outcome. In short, learning outcomes provide the focus that lessons need.

UNIT 6

Unit QUESTION
Who makes you laugh?

Laughter

LISTENING • listening for specific information
VOCABULARY • synonyms
GRAMMAR • simple present for informal narratives
PRONUNCIATION • simple present third-person -s/-es
SPEAKING • using eye contact, pause, and tone of voice

LEARNING OUTCOME
Use appropriate eye contact, tone of voice, and pauses to tell a funny story or a joke to your classmates.

In this example unit, students are asked to think about who makes them laugh while preparing to tell their own joke or funny story.

The unit assignment ties into that unit's unique learning outcome.

Tell a Story or Joke	20 points	15 points	10 points	0 points
Student told the joke or funny story easily (without long pauses or reading) and was easy to understand (spoke clearly and at a good speed).				
Student used the simple present tense correctly.				
Student used vocabulary from the unit.				
Student used eye contact, pauses, and tone of voice to effectively tell the joke or funny story.				
Student correctly pronounced third person -s/-es.				

Total points: _____

Comments:

Clear assessments allow both teachers and students to comment on and measure learner outcomes.

Q Unit Assignment: Tell a joke or a funny story

Unit Question (5 minutes)

Refer students back to the ideas they discussed at the beginning of the unit about who makes them laugh. Cue students if necessary by asking specific questions about the content of the unit: *Why did people think Jackie Chan was funny? What advice did we hear about how to be funny? What skills can you use to make your jokes and stories more entertaining?*

Learning Outcome

1. Tie the Unit Assignment to the unit learning outcome. Say: *The outcome for this unit is to use appropriate eye contact, tone of voice, and pauses to tell a funny story or a joke to your classmates. This Unit Assignment is going to let you show that you can do that as well as correctly use and pronounce the simple present.*

CRITICAL THINKING

A critical thinking approach asks students to process new information and to learn how to apply that information to a new situation. Teachers might set learning outcomes to give students targets to hit—for example: "After this lesson, give three reasons why people immigrate"—and the materials and exercises in the lesson provide students with the knowledge and skills to think critically and discover *their* three reasons.

Questions are important catalysts in the critical thinking process. Questions encourage students to reflect on and apply their knowledge to new situations. Students and teachers work together to understand, analyze, synthesize, and evaluate the lesson's questions and content to reach the stated outcomes. As students become more familiar with these stages of the critical thinking process, they will be able to use new information to complete tasks more efficiently and in unique and meaningful ways.

Tip) Critical Thinking

In Activity B, you have to **restate**, or say again in perhaps a different way, some of the information you learned in the two readings. **Restating** is a good way to review information.

> Throughout the Student Book, *Critical Thinking Tips* accompany certain activities, helping students to practice and understand these critical thinking skills.

B (10 minutes)

1. Introduce the Unit Question, *Why do people immigrate to other countries?* Ask related information questions or questions about personal experience to help students prepare for answering the more abstract unit question: *Did you immigrate to this country? What were your reasons for leaving your home country? What were your reasons for choosing your new country? What did you bring with you?*

2. Tell students: *Let's start off our discussion by listing reasons why people might immigrate. For example, we could start our list with* finding work *because many people look for jobs in new countries. But there are many other reasons why people immigrate. What else can we think of?*

Critical Thinking Tip (1 minute)

1. Read the tip aloud.

2. Tell students that restating also helps to ensure that they have understood something correctly. After reading a new piece of information, they should try to restate it to a classmate who has also read the information, to ensure that they both have the same understanding of information.

> The *Q Teacher's Handbook* features notes offering questions for expanded thought and discussion.

CRITICAL Q EXPANSION ACTIVITIES

The *Q Teacher's Handbook* expands on the critical thinking approach with the Critical Q Expansion Activities. These activities allow teachers to facilitate more practice for their students. The Critical Q Expansion Activities supplement the *Q Student Book* by expanding on skills and language students are practicing.

In today's classrooms, it's necessary that students have the ability to apply the skills they have learned to new situations with materials they have never seen before. Q's focus on critical thinking and the *Q Teacher's Handbook's* emphasis on practicing critical thinking skills through the Critical Q Expansion Activities prepares students to excel in this important skill.

> The easy-to-use activity suggestions increase student practice and success with critical thinking skills.

Critical Q: Expansion Activity

Outlining

1. Explain to students: *A popular way to prepare to outline one's ideas is to use a cluster map. In a cluster map, a big circle is drawn in the middle of a page or on the board, and a main point is written inside it—**this will become the topic sentence in the outline.***

2. Then explain: *Next, lines are drawn away from the circle and new, smaller circles are attached to the other end of those lines. Inside each of the smaller circles, ideas are written which relate to the main point—**these become supporting sentences in the outline.***

Both the academic and professional worlds are becoming increasingly interdependent. The toughest problems are solved only when looked at from multiple perspectives. Success in the 21ˢᵗ century requires more than just core academic knowledge—though that is still crucial. Now, successful students have to collaborate, innovate, adapt, be self-directed, be flexible, be creative, be tech-literate, practice teamwork, and be accountable—both individually and in groups.

Q approaches language learning in light of these important 21ˢᵗ Century Skills. Each unit asks students to practice many of these attributes, from collaboration to innovation to accountability, *while* they are learning new language and content. The *Q Student Books* focus on these increasingly important skills with unique team, pair, and individual activities. Additionally, the *Q Teacher's Handbooks* provide support with easy-to-use 21ˢᵗ Century Skill sections for teachers who want to incorporate skills like "openness to other people's ideas and opinions" into their classrooms but aren't sure where to start.

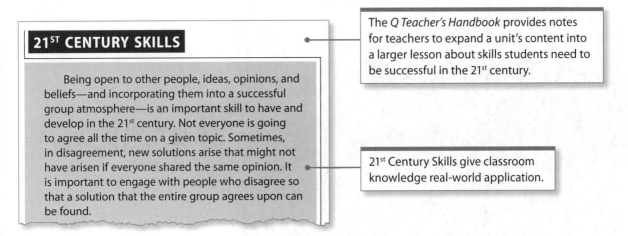

21ˢᵀ CENTURY SKILLS

Being open to other people, ideas, opinions, and beliefs—and incorporating them into a successful group atmosphere—is an important skill to have and develop in the 21ˢᵗ century. Not everyone is going to agree all the time on a given topic. Sometimes, in disagreement, new solutions arise that might not have arisen if everyone shared the same opinion. It is important to engage with people who disagree so that a solution that the entire group agrees upon can be found.

The *Q Teacher's Handbook* provides notes for teachers to expand a unit's content into a larger lesson about skills students need to be successful in the 21ˢᵗ century.

21ˢᵗ Century Skills give classroom knowledge real-world application.

Q ONLINE PRACTICE

Q Online Practice is an online workbook that gives students quick access to all-new content in a range of additional practice activities. The interface is intuitive and user-friendly, allowing students to focus on enhancing their language skills.

For the teacher, *Q Online Practice* includes a digital grade book providing immediate and accurate assessment of each student's progress. Straightforward individual student or class reports can be viewed onscreen, printed, or exported, giving you comprehensive feedback on what students have mastered or where they need more help.

Teacher's Access Code Cards for the digital grade book are available upon adoption or for purchase. Use the access code to register for your *Q Online Practice* account at www.Qonlinepractice.com.

These features of the *Q: Skills for Success* series enable you to help your students develop the skills they need to succeed in their future academic and professional careers. By using learning outcomes, critical thinking, and 21ˢᵗ century skills, you help students gain a deeper knowledge of the material they are presented with, both in and out of the classroom.

Q connects critical thinking, language skills, and learning outcomes.

LANGUAGE SKILLS

Explicit skills instruction enables students to meet their academic and professional goals.

LEARNING OUTCOMES

Clearly identified **learning outcomes** focus students on the goal of their instruction.

UNIT 6

The Science of Food

LISTENING	understanding bias in a presentation
VOCABULARY	prefixes and suffixes
GRAMMAR	comparative forms of adjectives and adverbs
PRONUNCIATION	common intonation patterns
SPEAKING	expressing interest during a conversation

LEARNING OUTCOME

Participate in a debate on food science, stating and supporting your opinions about food modification.

Unit QUESTION

How has science changed the food we eat?

PREVIEW THE UNIT

Ⓐ **Discuss these questions with your classmates.**

Which is more important in the food you choose: flavor, cost, or nutrition? Why?

Scientists have developed ways to genetically modify plants. What do you know about genetically modified food?

Look at the photo. How have the tomatoes been modified? Would you want to try them?

Ⓑ **Discuss the Unit Question with your classmates.**

Listen to *The Q Classroom*, Track 24 on CD 2, to hear other answers.

108   UNIT 6

109

CRITICAL THINKING

Thought-provoking **unit questions** engage students with the topic and provide a **critical thinking framework** for the unit.

 Having the learning outcome is important because it gives students and teachers a clear idea of what the point of each task/activity in the unit is.
Lawrence Lawson, Palomar College, California

PREVIEW LISTENING 1

LANGUAGE SKILLS

Two listening texts provide input on the unit question and give **exposure to academic content.**

Food Additives Linked to Hyperactivity in Kids

You are going to listen to a radio report about food chemicals and their effects on children's behavior.

Work with a partner. Why might chemicals in food affect a child's behavior? Give reasons for your answer.

CRITICAL THINKING

Students **discuss** their opinions of each listening text and **analyze** how it changes their perspective on the unit question.

Q WHAT DO YOU THINK?

A. Discuss the questions in a group.

1. Some genetically altered plants need less water to grow, are resistant to insects, or are more nutritious. Farmers may be able to feed more people by growing genetically modified crops. Do the benefits of growing genetically modified crops outweigh possible risks? Give reasons for your answer.

2. In some countries, genetically altered foods must have a label explaining that they are altered. Is this law a good idea? Why or why not?

B. Think about both Listening 1 and Listening 2 as you discuss the questions.

Do you know if any foods you eat have been genetically modified? Do you know which foods contain additives? How can you find out? How will this information affect what you buy?

 One of the best features is your focus on developing materials of a high "interest level."
Troy Hammond, Tokyo Gakugei University, International Secondary School, Japan

Explicit skills instruction prepares students for academic success.

LANGUAGE SKILLS

Explicit instruction and practice in listening, speaking, grammar, pronunciation, and vocabulary skills **help students achieve language proficiency.**

LEARNING OUTCOMES

Practice activities allow students to **master the skills** before they are evaluated at the end of the unit.

Listening Skill | Understanding bias in a presentation

Bias is a strong feeling for or against something. Understanding the bias in a presentation is important. Speakers may express biases even when they're trying to sound objective. In Listening 1, the speaker presents research both for and against a link between food additives and hyperactivity, but the speaker's bias appears to be against food additives.

There are several clues to help you understand the bias of a presentation.

Title: Listening 1 is "Food Additives Linked to Hyperactivity in Kids." This is a negative idea, and it sounds very definite. This probably means the speaker agrees with the research in the report. A different title, such as "Some Researchers Believe Food Additives May Affect Hyperactivity" does not show such a strong bias.

Introduction: Pay attention to how a speaker introduces a topic. For example, if a speaker starts with, *I'm going to talk about the negative effects of food additives on children's behavior,* that statement alone tells you the speaker's bias.

Imbalance: Reports with a bias usually report on both sides of the issue, but the information is not balanced well. In Listening 1, most of the report is about the research results that show a link between additives and hyperactivity, and only a small part of the report is about research that doesn't show any link.

Information source: Consider who is providing the information. For example, suppose a company that sells chocolate presents research that shows eating chocolate is good for you. Knowing the company sells chocolate can help you decide how much to trust the information.

🔊 CD 2 Track 27 **A. Listen to the short report. Then answer the questions.**

1. Check (✓) the clues you hear that tell you the bias.

☐ Title
☐ Introduction
☐ Imbalance
☐ Information source

2. Is the speaker against organic food or in favor of organic food?

_____

🔊 CD 2 Track 28 **B. Listen to excerpts from four news reports. What bias is being shown in each report? Circle the correct answer.**

Excerpt 1

a. Some scientists believe there are many causes of obesity.

b. Some scientists believe fast food is the main cause of obesity.

Tip for Success

When you listen to the radio, focus on the speakers' intonation. Pay attention to how they use their voices to express ideas and emotions.

B. Work with a partner. Take turns asking and answering the questions. Ask follow-up questions if needed. Focus on using the correct intonation.

1. What are your favorite foods?

2. What is the strangest food you have ever eaten?

3. What are three foods you would never try?

4. Who usually cooks at your house?

Speaking Skill | Expressing interest during a conversation

Expressing interest during a conversation shows the speaker you are paying attention. There are several ways to express interest in the speaker's ideas. In addition to leaning forward and making eye contact, you can use special words and phrases to show you are interested.

Encouraging words: Yeah. / Wow! / Mm-hmm. / Cool!
Comments: How interesting! / That's amazing!
Emphasis questions: Really?
Repeating words: Speaker: I went to Paris. You: Oh, Paris!

It is not necessary to wait until the speaker has finished talking to use these words and phrases. You can use them throughout the conversation, whenever the speaker completes a thought.

🔊 CD 2 Track 33 **A. Listen to the conversation between two students who are eating lunch. Fill in the blanks with the words in the box. Then practice the conversation with a partner.**

| mm-hmm | that's interesting | wow |
| really | every day | yeah |

Noriko: Hey, Marc. Is this seat free? Do you mind if I sit here?

Marc: Not at all. How are you doing?

Noriko: I'm absolutely starving!

Marc: _____? Why?

Noriko: I went to the gym this morning before school, and by 11:00, my stomach was growling in class.

Marc: _____, that had to be embarrassing.

 The tasks are simple, accessible, user-friendly, and very useful.
Jessica March, American University of Sharjah, U.A.E.

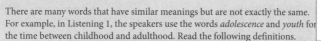

LEARNER CENTERED

Q Online Practice provides all new content for additional practice in an easy-to-use online workbook. Every student book includes a *Q Online Practice access code card*. Use the access code to register for your *Q Online Practice* account at www.Qonlinepractice.com.

Vocabulary Skill Using the dictionary web⁺

There are many words that have similar meanings but are not exactly the same. For example, in Listening 1, the speakers use the words *adolescence* and *youth* for the time between childhood and adulthood. Read the following definitions.

ad·o·les·cence /ˌædlˈɛsns/ *noun* [U] the time in a person's life when he or she develops from a child into an adult **SYN** PUBERTY ⊃ collocations at AGE

youth /yuθ/ *noun* (pl. youths /yuðz; yuθs/) **1** [U] the time of life when a person is young, especially the time before a child becomes an adult: *He had been a talented musician in his youth.*

The dictionary definitions show that although the words are very similar, *adolescence* describes a more specific time period, while *youth* is more general.

Checking the definitions of similar words can help you determine which word is appropriate in a context.

All dictionary entries are taken from the *Oxford Advanced American Dictionary for learners of English.*

LANGUAGE SKILLS

A **research-based vocabulary program** focuses students on the words they need to know academically and professionally, using skill strategies based on the same research as the Oxford dictionaries.

All dictionary entries are taken from the *Oxford Advanced American Dictionary for learners of English.*

The *Oxford Advanced American Dictionary for learners of English* was developed with English learners in mind, and provides extra learning tools for pronunciation, verb types, basic grammar structures, and more.

The Oxford 3000™ 🔑
The Oxford 3000 encompasses **the 3000 most important words to learn in English.** It is based on a comprehensive analysis of the Oxford English Corpus, a two-billion word collection of English text, and on extensive research with both language and pedagogical experts.

The Academic Word List **AWL**
The Academic Word List was created by Averil Coxhead and contains **570 words that are commonly used in academic English,** such as in textbooks or articles across a wide range of academic subject areas. These words are a great place to start if you are studying English for academic purposes.

Clear learning outcomes focus students on the goals of instruction.

Unit Assignment	Persuade a group

 In this section, you are going to present your opinion to persuade a group of people. As you prepare your presentation, think about the Unit Question, "How can we maintain a balance with nature?" and refer to the Self-Assessment checklist on page 196.

For alternative unit assignments, see the *Q: Skills for Success Teacher's Handbook.*

CONSIDER THE IDEAS

 CD 4 Track 11

A. Listen to a news report about the situation in a small town. Think about the questions as you listen.

1. Why does Spring Hill need to develop the land near the lake?

2. What are the concerns about developing the land?

3. What outcome does the mayor hope the town hall meeting will produce?

Check (✓) the skills you learned. If you need more work on a skill, refer to the page(s) in parentheses.

LISTENING	I can understand bias in a presentation. (p. 114)
VOCABULARY	I can recognize and use prefixes and suffixes. (pp. 118–119)
GRAMMAR	I can use comparative forms of adjectives and adverbs. (p. 120)
PRONUNCIATION	I can use common intonation patterns. (p. 122)
SPEAKING	I can express interest during a conversation. (p. 123)
LEARNING OUTCOME	I can participate in a debate on food science, stating and supporting my opinions about food modification.

 Students can check their learning . . . and they can focus on the essential points when they study.

Suh Yoomi, Seoul, South Korea

Q Online Practice

For the student

- **Easy-to-use:** a simple interface allows students to focus on enhancing their speaking and listening skills, not learning a new software program
- **Flexible:** for use anywhere there's an Internet connection
- **Access code card:** a *Q Online Practice* access code is included with the student book—Use the access code to register for *Q Online Practice* at www.Qonlinepractice.com

For the teacher

- **Simple yet powerful:** automatically grades student exercises and tracks progress
- **Straightforward:** online management system to review, print, or export reports
- **Flexible:** for use in the classroom or easily assigned as homework
- **Access code card:** contact your sales rep for your *Q Online Practice* teacher's access code

Teacher Resources

Q Teacher's Handbook gives strategic support through:
- specific teaching notes for each activity
- ideas for ensuring student participation
- multilevel strategies and expansion activities
- the answer key
- special sections on 21st century skills and critical thinking
- a *Testing Program CD-ROM* with a customizable test for each unit

Oxford
Teachers' Club

For additional resources visit the
Q: Skills for Success companion website at
www.oup.com/elt/teacher/Qskillsforsuccess

Q Class Audio includes:
- listening texts
- pronunciation presentations and exercises
- *The Q Classroom*

> " It's an interesting, engaging series which provides plenty of materials that are easy to use in class, as well as instructionally promising. "
> *Donald Weasenforth, Collin College, Texas*

UNIT	LISTENING	SPEAKING	VOCABULARY
1 Power and Responsibility **How does power affect leaders?** **LISTENING 1: Best of Both Worlds?** A Report (Business Management) **LISTENING 2: Myths of Effective Leadership** A Lecture (Human Resources Management)	• Listen for expressions that announce a topic to anticipate what you will hear • Listen to results of a study in order to understand evidence • Distinguish stressed and unstressed syllables to better identify words in speech • Predict content • Listen for main ideas • Listen for details	• Use repetition and signal words to draw attention to main ideas • Discuss a reading with group members to analyze the author's points • Take notes to prepare for a presentation or group discussion	• Understand the meaning of new vocabulary from context
2 Appearances **How does appearance affect our success?** **LISTENING 1: A Perfect Mess** A Book Review (Psychology) **LISTENING 2: The Changing Business Dress Code** An Interview (Fashion design)	• Identify new and previously known information to focus on important details • Decide which information to take notes on so note-taking is efficient • Listen for unstressed vowels to recognize individual words in speech • Predict content • Listen for main ideas • Listen for details	• Confirm that you understand what another has said • Give another person advice to help handle a difficult situation • Take notes to prepare for a presentation or group discussion	• Find the relevant definition for a multi-meaning word in the dictionary • Assess your prior knowledge of vocabulary
3 Growing Up **When does a child become an adult?** **LISTENING 1: Generation Next** A Radio Report (Cultural Anthropology) **LISTENING 2: Growing Up Quickly** A Lecture (Developmental Psychology)	• Pay attention to titles, previous experience, etc. to anticipate information • Listen for key words to understand who is performing an action • Predict content • Listen for main ideas • Listen for details	• Give individual and small-group presentations to define a term and explain it • Stress important words in speech to communicate important information • Brainstorm ideas to prepare for presentations • Take notes to prepare for a presentation or group discussion	• Use the dictionary to distinguish between words with similar meanings • Assess your prior knowledge of vocabulary

GRAMMAR	PRONUNCIATION	CRITICAL THINKING	UNIT OUTCOME
• Gerunds and infinitives	• Syllable stress	• Examine personal attitudes toward leadership • Distinguish between truth and myths • Discuss research findings and evidence • Assess your prior knowledge of content • Relate personal experiences to listening topics • Integrate information from multiple sources	• Give a presentation about effective leadership and how to avoid the negative effects of power.
• Subjunctive verbs for suggestions	• Syllables with unstressed vowels (represented by the schwa)	• Examine factors involved in personal success • Formulate advice for others • Infer meaning from photographs • Assess your prior knowledge of content • Relate personal experiences to listening topics • Integrate information from multiple sources	• Role-play a conversation offering advice to help someone become better organized.
• Transitive and intransitive phrasal verbs	• Patterns of stress in sentences	• Become aware of personal behavior in social contexts • Apply criteria to classify individual circumstances • Identify cultural norms and compare them with those of other eras • Assess your prior knowledge of content • Relate personal experiences to listening topics • Integrate information from multiple sources	• Present a personal story describing an important event in your life that made you feel like an adult.

UNIT	LISTENING	SPEAKING	VOCABULARY
4 Health Care **How is health care changing?** **LISTENING 1:** Vacation, Adventure, and Surgery? A News Report (Public Health) **LISTENING 2:** Medical Travel Can Create Problems A Report (Public Policy)	• Listen for reasons to better understand the views and actions of others • Listen for numbers to better understand circumstances • Distinguish between similar-sounding words to understand exactly what a speaker says • Predict content • Listen for main ideas • Listen for details	• Ask open-ended and follow-up questions to get information and to keep a conversation going • Interview others to discover widespread trends • Take notes to prepare for a presentation or group discussion	• Learn and remember collocations of verbs with nouns • Assess your prior knowledge of vocabulary
5 Art Today **What makes a work of art popular?** **LISTENING 1:** Manga's New Popularity A Radio Report (Art) **LISTENING 2:** Thomas Kinkade A Report (Aesthetics)	• Make inferences to more fully understand what someone says • Recognize the meaning of speed, pitch, and tone • Predict content • Listen for main ideas • Listen for details	• Avoid answering questions to keep certain information out of a conversation • Take notes to prepare for a presentation or group discussion	• Recognize and produce word forms for different parts of speech • Assess your prior knowledge of vocabulary
6 The Science of Food **How has science changed the food we eat?** **LISTENING 1:** Food Additives Linked to Hyperactivity in Kids A Radio Report (Nutrition) **LISTENING 2:** The "Flavr Savr" Tomato A News Report (Agriculture and Genetics)	• Understand a speaker's bias to put information into perspective • Listen for examples to better understand general statements • Predict content • Listen for main ideas • Listen for details	• Express interest during a conversation to encourage the speaker to continue • Use rising intonation to indicate attitudes and purposes • Take notes to prepare for a presentation or group discussion	• Understand prefixes and suffixes • Assess your prior knowledge of vocabulary
7 From School to Work **Is one road to success better than another?** **LISTENING 1:** Changing Ways to Climb the Ladder A College Lecture (Business Management) **LISTENING 2:** Life Experience Before College A Radio Program (Career Counseling)	• Listen for contrasts to understand relationships of ideas • Listen for specific words or phrases to complete a transcript • Predict content • Listen for main ideas • Listen for details	• Change the topic to move a conversation into a comfortable area • Talk about real and unreal conditions to speculate about choices • Take notes to prepare for a presentation or group discussion	• Use the dictionary to determine how formal or informal a vocabulary item is • Assess your prior knowledge of vocabulary

GRAMMAR	PRONUNCIATION	CRITICAL THINKING	UNIT OUTCOME
• Past unreal conditionals	• *Can* and *can't*	• Identify desirable characteristics for professionals • Evaluate possible courses of action • Speculate about what might have happened under certain conditions • Assess your prior knowledge of content • Relate personal experiences to listening topics • Integrate information from multiple sources	• Participate in an interview about the advantages and disadvantages of medical tourism.
• Present perfect and present perfect continuous	• Basic intonation patterns	• Contrast individuals' tastes • Infer meanings from what a speaker chooses not to say • Judge the truth and relevance of traditional wisdom • Assess your prior knowledge of content • Relate personal experiences to listening topics • Integrate information from multiple sources	• Role-play a conversation expressing personal opinions about what makes art popular.
• Comparative forms of adjectives and adverbs	• More intonation patterns	• Describe personal tastes and habits • Integrate ideas from several sources • Examine the implications of scientific achievements • Show polite interest in a conversation • Assess your prior knowledge of content • Relate personal experiences to listening topics • Integrate information from multiple sources	• Participate in a debate on food science, stating and supporting your opinions about food modification.
• Simple, compound, and complex sentences	• Stress to highlight important words	• Match personal qualities with career requirements • Evaluate alternative paths for personal growth • Classify information • Assess your prior knowledge of content • Relate personal experiences to listening topics • Integrate information from multiple sources	• Participate in a group discussion about qualifications of job applicants and arrive at a hiring decision.

UNIT	LISTENING	SPEAKING	VOCABULARY
8 Discovery **How can chance discoveries affect our lives?** **LISTENING 1:** The Power of Serendipity A Report (History of Science) **LISTENING 2:** Against All Odds, Twin Girls Reunited A Report (Psychology)	• Listen for signal words and phrases to understand the structure of a listening passage • Listen for reasons and methods to understand a narrative • Recognize vowel linkages to distinguish words a speaker uses • Predict content • Listen for main ideas • Listen for details	• Use questions to maintain listener interest • Use direct and indirect quotations to report information from sources • Take notes to prepare for a presentation or group discussion	• Learn and remember collocations involving prepositions • Assess your prior knowledge of vocabulary
9 Humans and Nature **How can we maintain a balance with nature?** **LISTENING 1:** Polar Bears at Risk A Report (Ecology) **LISTENING 2:** The Effects of Oil Spills A Lecture (Climatology)	• Listen carefully to an introduction to prepare for upcoming information • Recognize vocabulary patterns in a listening passage • Listen for specific words and phrases to complete a transcript • Predict content • Listen for main ideas • Listen for details	• Use persuasive language to encourage positive attitudes toward your positions • Use reduced forms of pronouns and verbs to achieve a proper tone • Take notes to prepare for a presentation or group discussion	• Add suffixes to change word forms • Assess your prior knowledge of vocabulary
10 Child's Play **Is athletic competition good for children?** **LISTENING 1:** Training Chinese Athletes An Interview (Child Development) **LISTENING 2:** *Until It Hurts* Discusses Youth Sports Obsession A Book Discussion (Sports Medicine)	• Listen for causes and effects to understand relationships among ideas • Listen for opinions to match them with the people who hold them • Recognize idioms to understand a speaker's true meaning • Predict content • Listen for main ideas • Listen for details	• Add to a speaker's comments to become an active conversation partner • Use thought groups to segment sentences into understandable pieces • Take notes to prepare for a presentation or group discussion	• Understand idioms to avoid confusion about a speaker's true meaning • Assess your prior knowledge of vocabulary

GRAMMAR	PRONUNCIATION	CRITICAL THINKING	UNIT OUTCOME
• Structures for indirect speech	• Linked words with vowels	• Trace the origins of familiar objects • Examine the role of chance in daily events • Assess the significance of an item's characteristics • Assess your prior knowledge of content • Relate personal experiences to listening topics • Integrate information from multiple sources	• Recount the events involved in a personal discovery you made accidently and tell how it affected you.
• Relative clauses	• Reduced forms	• Determine causes and effects • Apply information about distant events to your own circumstances • Assess your prior knowledge of content • Relate personal experiences to listening topics • Integrate information from multiple sources	• Role-play a meeting in which you present and defend an opinion in order to persuade others.
• Real conditionals	• Thought groups	• Compare cultural approaches to personal development • Associate causes with effects • Evaluate the effectiveness of different training regimens • Assess your prior knowledge of content • Relate personal experiences to listening topics • Integrate information from multiple sources	• Participate in a group discussion about how to encourage children to exhibit good sportsmanship.

Unit QUESTION
How does power affect leaders?

Power and Responsibility

LISTENING • listening for main ideas
VOCABULARY • meaning from context
GRAMMAR • gerunds and infinitives
PRONUNCIATION • syllable stress
SPEAKING • checking for understanding

LEARNING OUTCOME

Give a presentation about effective leadership and how to avoid the negative effects of power.

▶ *Listening and Speaking 4, page 3*
Preview the Unit

Learning Outcome

1. Ask a volunteer to read the unit skills and then the unit learning outcome.

2. Explain: *This is what you are expected to be able to do by the unit's end. The learning outcome explains how you are going to be evaluated. With this outcome in mind, you should focus on learning these skills (Listening, Vocabulary, Grammar, Pronunciation, Speaking) that will support your goal of giving a presentation about effective leadership and how to avoid the negative effects of power. This can also help you act as mentors in the classroom to help the other students meet this outcome.*

A (15 minutes)

1. Elicit ideas about what it means to be a leader and write them on the board. For example: *being the boss, having people listen to me,* or *taking responsibility for a group's actions.* Alternatively, have students write their ideas on the board themselves.

2. Put students in pairs or small groups to discuss the first two questions.

3. Call on volunteers to share their ideas with the class. Ask: *What makes a good leader? Do you know any good leaders?* Point out that not all leaders have titles (like *boss* or *captain*).

4. Focus students' attention on the photo. Have a volunteer describe the photo to the class. Read the final question aloud. Elicit students' answers.

Activity A Answers, p. 3
Answers will vary. Possible answers:
1. I was the captain of my sports team. It was difficult because I had a lot of responsibility.
2. My company's president is a good leader because he takes care of everyone who works for him.
3. I see a statue of an important man. I think this man was a leader. I see a boy making a speech. Leaders often have to give speeches.

B (15 minutes)

1. Introduce the Unit Question, *How does power affect leaders?* Ask related information questions or questions about personal experience to help students prepare for answering the more abstract Unit Question. Ask: *What is power? Have you ever had power before? If so, how did it affect you? Do people change when they have power? How do they change?*

2. Put students in small groups and give each group a piece of poster paper and a marker.

3. Read the Unit Question aloud. Give students a minute to silently consider their answers to the question. Tell students to pass the paper and marker around the group. Direct each group member to write a different answer to the question. Encourage them to help one another.

4. Ask each group to choose a reporter to read the answers to the class. Point out similarities and differences among the answers. Make a group list that incorporates the most common answers. Post the list so students can refer to it later in the unit.

Answers will vary. Possible answers: Power makes leaders greedy. / Power helps leaders do the things they want to do to help people. / Leaders sometimes abuse the power they have.

The Q Classroom
🔊 CD1, Track 2

1. Play The Q Classroom. Use the example from the audio to help students continue the conversation. Ask: *How did the students answer the question?*

2. Yuna says that leaders feel more responsible when they have power. Ask: *Do you agree with Yuna? Why or why not?*

▶ *Listening and Speaking 4, page 4*

C (10 minutes)

1. Review the directions and characteristics as a class.

2. Have students check the three characteristics that they find to be most important. Then pair students to share their answers.

3. Put pairs into larger groups of four to share their answers. Have students focus on the characteristics they all chose. Ask: *Why do you think this characteristic is so important?*

D (10 minutes)

1. Put students into groups to discuss the questions.

2. Circulate around the classroom and note any incorrect language that you hear. Save the notes— two or three phrases or words—until later.

3. Ask volunteers to share their answers to the questions. Encourage students to comment on their classmates' ideas.

4. Write the incorrect words or phrases on the board. Explain that you heard these while you were listening to their conversations.

5. Ask students to try to correct them. Lead the class through the corrections so that students are clear about the correct forms/uses of the phrases or words.

▶ *Listening and Speaking 4, page 5*

LISTENING

LISTENING 1: Best of Both Worlds?

VOCABULARY (20 minutes)

1. Write the bold vocabulary words on board. When writing the verbs, use the infinitive form. Ask: *What words do you already know? What do those words mean?*

2. Ask students to read the words and definitions. Answer any questions about meaning and provide examples of the words in context.

3. Model pronunciation of the vocabulary words. Have students repeat.

4. Put students in pairs and have them complete the activity.

5. Ask volunteers to read the completed sentences. Correct any errors as a class.

MULTILEVEL OPTION

Group lower-level students and assist them with the task. Provide alternate example sentences to help them understand the words. For example: *One **aspect** of the class that I enjoy is listening practice. Every person has the **potential** to be a great leader.*

Have higher-level students complete the activity individually and then compare answers with a partner. Tell the pairs to write an additional sentence for each word. Have volunteers write one of their sentences on the board. Correct them as a class.

Vocabulary Answers, pp. 5–6
1. criticism; **2.** favoritism; **3.** acknowledge;
4. potential; **5.** aspect; **6.** expert;
7. staff; **8.** negotiate; **9.** outline;
10. address; **11.** exemplify; **12.** issue

 For additional practice with the vocabulary, have students visit *Q Online Practice*.

▶ *Listening and Speaking 4, page 6*

PREVIEW LISTENING 1 (10 minutes)

1. Write the title of the listening on the board. Have a volunteer read the introduction aloud. Have students discuss the question in pairs.

2. Tell students they should review their answers after listening because their answers may change.

Answers will vary. Possible answers: I think that they have to stop being friends because the boss cannot treat his or her friend fairly. / I think that they can continue to be friends because it's possible to be friends in a professional situation.

Listening 1 Background Note

Sometimes friends in the workplace find themselves in an unfamiliar situation when one of them is suddenly promoted to be the other's boss. Because promotions can put a strain on personal relationships, experts and career consultants offer advice on what to do when your friend becomes your boss. Some of their tips include:

- Try to keep your expectations reasonable. Accept that things have changed and your relationship will be different.

- Approach the situation as an opportunity to learn from someone you respect.

- Make sure to maintain confidentiality and keep any past conversations between you and your friend to yourself.

- Don't "flaunt" your friendship or act like you have special access to the boss. Other coworkers may become resentful.

- Make it a rule to not talk about work away from the office. Remember that your friend is now your superior.

- Support your friend and be there for him or her. After all, your friend will be dealing with a new set of responsibilities and pressures.

Even though you can't control the fact that your friend is now your boss, you do have control over how you react. Experts say that such a situation is the right time to show how good of a friend you are.

LISTEN FOR MAIN IDEAS (10 minutes)

CD1, Track 3

1. Preview the statements with students. Point out that in this activity, students will practice finding the main ideas of a listening.

2. Play the audio and have students label the statements *T* or *F*.

3. Read each statement. Have students raise their left hand for *False* and their right hand for *True*. Elicit corrections for the false statements.

Listen for Main Ideas Answers, p. 6
1. F; **2.** T; **3.** F; **4.** T

▶ *Listening and Speaking 4, page 7*
LISTEN FOR DETAILS (15 minutes)

CD1, Track 4

1. Direct students to read the sentences and answer choices.

2. Play the audio and have students complete the activity.

3. Have students compare answers with a partner. Play the audio again if necessary.

4. Go over the answers with the class.

Listen for Details Answers, p. 7
1. b; **2.** a; **3.** b; **4.** c

For additional practice with listening for details, have students visit *Q Online Practice*.

WHAT DO YOU THINK? (15 minutes)

1. Ask students to read the questions and reflect on their answers.

2. Seat students in small groups and assign roles: a group leader to make sure everyone contributes, a note-taker to record the group's ideas, a reporter to share the group's ideas with the class, and a timekeeper to watch the clock.

3. Give students ten minutes to discuss the questions. Call time if conversations are winding down. Allow extra time if necessary.

4. Call on each group's reporter to share ideas with the class.

What Do You Think? Answers, p. 7
Answers will vary. Possible answers:
1. If you hire a friend, you already know the person's skills and strengths.
2. I would not hire my closest friend because I think that being my friend's boss would change our relationship in a negative way. / I would hire my friend because I know that our personalities are similar.
3. I don't think my relationship with my friend would change because we are able to separate business from friendship.

▶ *Listening and Speaking 4, page 8*

Listening Skill: Listening for main ideas (20 minutes)

1. Remind students that the main ideas of a text or listening are the most important ideas.

2. Read the information about listening for main ideas. Point out the phrases that are used to introduce main ideas. Tell students that when they listen, if they hear an idea that is repeated several times, it is likely to be a main idea.

A (10 minutes)

1. Ask a student to read the directions aloud. Have students complete the activity individually.

2. Check the answers as a class.

3. Identify the repeated ideas in each presentation that helped students determine the main idea.

> **Activity A Answers, pp. 8–9**
> **1.** b;   **2.** c;   **3.** b

▶ *Listening and Speaking 4, page 9*

B (15 minutes)
🔊 CD1, Track 5

1. Preview the chart. Then play the short presentation. As they listen, instruct students to take notes in the chart.

2. Ask students to pair up and compare notes. Play the audio again.

3. Elicit answers from volunteers. You may want to reproduce the chart on the board.

> **Activity B Answers, p. 9**
> Answers will vary. Possible answers:
> Topic: Building a successful business
> Most important factor: People
> First characteristic mentioned: People who understand your vision and share your commitment to it
> Second characteristic mentioned: Creative, independent thinkers
> Last characteristic mentioned: Willing to work hard

 For additional practice with listening for main ideas, have students visit *Q Online Practice*.

Learning Outcome

Use the learning outcome to frame the purpose and relevance of Listening 1. Ask: *What did you learn from Listening 1 that prepares you to give a presentation about effective leadership and how to avoid the negative effects of power?* (Students learned about the advantages and challenges of working with friends. They may want to refer to these ideas when they give their presentations.)

▶ *Listening and Speaking 4, page 10*

LISTENING 2:
Myths of Effective Leadership

VOCABULARY (20 minutes)

1. Ask students to read the words and their definitions. Answer any questions about meaning and provide examples of the words in context. Model the pronunciation of each word and have students repeat.

2. Have students fill in the blanks with the vocabulary words. Check the answers as a class.

3. List all ten vocabulary words in 2 or 3 columns on the board, leaving some space between words and columns.

4. Divide the class into as many groups as there are columns and line each group up at an equal distance from the board, in front of one of the columns.

5. Read one of the definitions. When you do, the first student in line from each group should "slap" the correct word. Make sure the word remains clear on the board after students have "slapped" it. Repeat for all of the vocabulary words.

> **Vocabulary Answers, pp. 10–11**
> **1.** capable;   **2.** style;   **3.** assess;
> **4.** advance;   **5.** perspective;   **6.** contact;
> **7.** ethical;   **8.** effective;   **9.** title;
> **10.** executive

MULTILEVEL OPTION

Have lower-level students rewrite the words that are "slapped" off the board. Have higher-level students give an example sentence with the word they "slap."

 For additional practice with the vocabulary, have students visit *Q Online Practice*.

▶ *Listening and Speaking 4, page 11*

PREVIEW LISTENING 2 (10 minutes)

1. Read aloud the title of Listening 2. Ask: *What is a myth? What myths do you know?*

2. Read the introduction. Pair students so they can complete the activity. Elicit ideas from volunteers.

3. Before they listen, ask students: *What skill have we learned that will help you understand this listening more easily?* (Listening for main ideas) *How can it help?*

4. Tell students they should review their ideas after listening.

Listening 2 Background Note

The Center for Creative Leadership (CCL) is a nonprofit, global organization that focuses on leadership education and research. Their mission is to understand, practice, and develop leadership for the benefit of individuals and organizations around the world.

CCL defines creative leadership as "the capacity to think and act beyond the boundaries that limit our effectiveness." Some of their key beliefs are that leaders are made, not born, and that they can adapt and change. The group also believes that effective leaders are those that have strong interpersonal skills, are self-aware, and are capable of personal reflection.

LISTEN FOR MAIN IDEAS (10 minutes)

CD1, Track 6

1. Preview the questions with students.

2. Play the podcast. Ask students to answer the questions individually.

3. Have students check their answers in pairs. Elicit the answers from volunteers.

> **Listen for Main Ideas Answers, p. 11**
> **1.** They see themselves as more intelligent and capable than those around them in the organization.
> **2.** They see those who disagree with them as less capable, less intelligent, and less ethical.
> **3.** They begin to see the executives as ineffective leaders. Those who disagree keep silent or leave the company.

▶ *Listening and Speaking 4, page 12*

LISTEN FOR DETAILS (15 minutes)

A (10 minutes)
CD1, Track 7

1. Direct students to read the six statements. Play the audio again and have students complete the activity.

2. Have students compare answers with a partner.

3. Go over the answers with the class.

> **Activity A Answers, p. 12**
> **1.** T; **2.** T; **3.** F; **4.** T; **5.** F; **6.** T

B (5 minutes)

1. Direct students to check the pieces of advice that the speaker offers to executives.

2. Have students compare answers with a partner.

3. Check the answers as a class.

> **Activity B Answers, p. 12**
> Checked: Find and listen to new ideas and perspectives; find someone who is willing to disagree with you; get some feedback that assesses your leadership style.

 For additional practice with listening for details, have students visit *Q Online Practice*.

WHAT DO YOU THINK?

A (15 minutes)

1. Ask students to read the questions and reflect on their answers.

2. Seat students in small groups and assign roles: a group leader to make sure everyone contributes, a note-taker to record the group's ideas, a reporter to share the group's ideas with the class, and a timekeeper to watch the clock.

3. Give students ten minutes to discuss the questions. Call time if conversations are winding down. Allow extra time if necessary.

4. Call on each group's reporter to share ideas with the class.

> **Activity A Answers, p. 12**
> Answers will vary. Possible answers:
> **1.** Leadership is the ability to help people meet certain goals. Power is the ability to get people to do what you want them to do.
> **2.** I think that this happens because it becomes easy, as a leader, to get other people to do things for you. Leaders blur the line because it makes their lives easier.

B (10 minutes)

1. Have students continue working in their small groups to discuss the questions in Activity B. Tell them to choose a new leader, note-taker, reporter, and timekeeper.

2. Call on the new reporter to share each group's answers to the questions.

> **Activity B Answers, p. 12**
> Answers will vary. Possible answers:
> 1. When someone has power, that person has the ability to make changes that will benefit others.
> 2. The most valuable piece of advice is to find a person who disagrees with your point of view. / I disagree with the advice to get feedback on your leadership style. Sometimes people don't feel comfortable criticizing a person with a lot of power, so leaders don't get the feedback they are looking for.

Learning Outcome

Use the learning outcome to frame the purpose and relevance of Listenings 1 and 2. Ask: *What did you learn from Listenings 1 and 2 that prepares you to give a presentation about effective leadership and how to avoid the negative effects of power?* (Students learned about working with friends and being an effective leader. They may want to refer to some of these ideas when they give their presentations.)

▶ *Listening and Speaking 4, page 13*

Vocabulary Skill: Understanding meaning from context (15 minutes)

1. Read the title of the Vocabulary Skill. Explain: *You can use the context of a sentence or paragraph to figure out what an unfamiliar word or phrase means.*

2. Read the first paragraph and example sentence. Write the sentence on the board. Elicit from students any context clues to the meaning of the word *promotion* and circle them. Then have a volunteer read the next paragraph.

3. Go through the second, longer example in the same way.

4. Check comprehension: *What can you do to figure out the meaning of a word you don't know? Should you look at just one sentence every time? Why or why not?*

Skill Note

As students learn new vocabulary words, have them look at the example sentences provided with the definitions in the dictionary. Some entries will have several different example sentences to show the different meanings of a word. These sentences will provide context and help students better understand what the word means.

A (10 minutes)

🔊 CD1, Track 8

1. Play the audio. Have students work individually to complete the activity. Then place students with partners to compare answers.

2. Go over the answers with the class.

> **Activity A Answers, p. 13**
> **1.** b; **2.** c; **3.** d; **4.** a; **5.** e

▶ *Listening and Speaking 4, page 14*

B (10 minutes)

🔊 CD1, Track 9

1. Have students preview the items.

2. Play the audio again, pausing after each item. Have students complete the activity individually.

3. Then check answers as a class.

> **Activity B Answers, p. 14**
> **1.** c; **2.** b; **3.** a; **4.** b; **5.** a

C (10 minutes)

1. Have students complete the activity individually and then read their sentences to a partner.

2. Ask a few volunteers to share their sentences with the class.

> **Activity C Answers, p. 14**
> Answers will vary.

> **MULTILEVEL OPTION**
>
> Have lower-level students work in pairs to write their sentences together. Ask higher-level students to write more than five sentences.

 For additional practice with understanding meaning from context, have students visit *Q Online Practice*.

▶ *Listening and Speaking 4, page 15*

SPEAKING

Grammar: Gerunds and infinitives
(15 minutes)

1. Read the title of the grammar skill. Ask: *Do you know what an infinitive is? Do you know what a gerund is?*

2. Go over the information in the box.

3. Check comprehension by asking questions: *What ending do gerunds have?* (-ing) *What types of words are gerunds used after?* (prepositions and verbs) *What two words make an infinitive?* (to + verb) *Which verbs are infinitives used after?*

4. Elicit additional example sentences with gerunds and infinitives.

A (10 minutes)

1. Read the directions aloud. Remind students that gerunds end in *–ing* and infinitives follow the formula *to* + verb.

2. Ask students to underline the gerunds and infinitives.

3. Go over the answers with the class.

> **Activity A Answers, p. 15**
> **1.** to hire; **2.** to understand; **3.** Knowing;
> **4.** Managing; **5.** saying; to be **6.** to be;
> **7.** taking

▶ *Listening and Speaking 4, page 16*

B (10 minutes)

1. Direct students to complete the activity individually, checking their answers with a partner once done. Remind them to look back at the skill box on page 15 for help.

2. Call on volunteers to read the completed sentences aloud.

> **Activity B Answers, p. 16**
> **1.** to finish; **2.** hiring; **3.** Working;
> **4.** to work; **5.** to communicate; **6.** discussing;
> **7.** to discuss; **8.** moving; to wait

 For additional practice with gerunds and infinitives, have students visit *Q Online Practice.*

Pronunciation: Syllable stress (15 minutes)

🔊 CD1, Track 10

1. Write a few words on the board (e.g., *English, discuss, recommend, effectively*). Ask students to determine how many syllables are in each word. Then elicit which syllable receives primary stress and mark it.

2. Go over the information in the skill box and play the audio clips when necessary.

3. Check comprehension by asking questions: *Which syllable is stressed in* negotiate? (go) *How does the stressed syllable sound different? When you learn a new word, what should you do?* (Learn the stress pattern of the word.)

Skill Note

There are a number of nouns that are also verbs that have different stress patterns (e.g., a *con*flict vs. to con*flict*; a *record* vs. to re*cord*). In two-syllable words, often the noun is stressed on the first syllable while the verb is stressed on the second syllable. Examples of words that fit this pattern are *address, contrast, present,* and *project.*

EXPANSION ACTIVITY: Nouns and Verbs (10 minutes)

1. Read the following list of words to students and have them determine if they are nouns or verbs: con*tract* (verb), *con*tract (noun); ob*ject* (verb), *ob*ject (noun); pro*duce* (verb), *pro*duce (noun).

2. Discuss the difference in meaning between the noun and verb forms.

3. Write the words *contract, object,* and *produce* on the board. Point to one, say *noun* or *verb,* and have students say the word with the stress on the correct syllable.

▶ *Listening and Speaking 4, page 17*

A (5 minutes)

🔊 CD1, Track 11

1. Play the audio. Direct students to circle the stressed syllable as they listen to the words.

2. Put students in pairs to check their answers.

3. Elicit the answers from volunteers.

> **Activity A Answers, p. 17**
> **1.** ex<u>cerpt</u>; **2.** <u>as</u>pect; **3.** en<u>force</u>;
> **4.** ef<u>fec</u>tive; **5.** <u>lea</u>dership; **6.** ac<u>know</u>ledge;
> **7.** per<u>spec</u>tive **8.** op<u>pos</u>ing; **9.** pro<u>mo</u>tion;
> **10.** inter<u>ac</u>tion

Tip for Success (5 minutes)

1. Read the tip aloud.

2. Have students look at a few dictionary entries and point out the pronunciation guide. Explain how to read and understand the pronunciation guide.

B (5 minutes)

 CD1, Track 12

1. Play the audio again.

2. Put students in pairs to practice pronouncing the words.

 For additional practice with syllable stress, have students visit *Q Online Practice*.

Speaking Skill: Checking for understanding (15 minutes)

1. Probe for previous knowledge. Ask: *When you have a conversation with someone, what can you say to check that the person understands what you mean?* Write students' ideas on the board.

2. Go over the information in the skill box.

3. Pair students up and have them practice saying the new phrases to each other.

▶ *Listening and Speaking 4, page 18*

A (10 minutes)

 CD1, Track 13

1. Have a volunteer read the directions aloud. Ask students to preview the phrases.

2. Play the audio track. Have students check the phrases the manager uses.

3. Go over the answers with the class.

> **Activity A Answers, p. 18**
> Checked: Do you know what I mean? Does everyone understand? Are you following me? Got it?

B (10 minutes)

 CD1, Track 14

1. Replay the audio. Have students take notes on the manager's main ideas.

2. Put students into pairs to compare their notes. Elicit the main points from volunteers.

> **Activity B Answers, p. 18**
> Answers will vary. Possible answers:
> We need to work extra hard. Drop other projects for now. Meet again today at 3:00 p.m.

 For additional practice with checking for understanding, have students visit *Q Online Practice*.

Critical Thinking Tip (2 minutes)

1. Read the Critical Thinking Tip aloud.

2. Remind students that the main points or ideas are often repeated. You may want to listen to the audio again to identify the repeated ideas.

Critical Q: Expansion Activity

Summarize

Tell students two personal stories, such as one about how you became a teacher and one about a person who you admire and why. As you speak, ask half the class to take notes on the main ideas in your first story. Ask the other half to take notes on the main points in your second story.

Place students into pairs so that each student has notes on the opposite story. Ask them to summarize what they heard using their notes. Circulate around the room to monitor how well students summarized your stories.

Ask students who you thought summarized your story well to share their summary with the class.

Unit Assignment: Offer advice on how to be an effective leader

Unit Question (5 minutes)

Refer students back to the ideas they discussed at the beginning of the unit about how power affects leaders. Cue students if necessary by asking specific questions about the content of the unit: *How does power change people? Are those changes positive or negative?* Read the directions for the assignment together.

Learning Outcome

1. Tie the Unit Assignment to the unit learning outcome. Say: *The outcome for this unit is to give a presentation about effective leadership and how to avoid the negative effects of power. This Unit Assignment is going to let you practice your speaking skills by offering advice on how to be an effective leader. You will also practice checking for understanding and using correct syllable stress.*

2. Explain that you are going to use a rubric similar to their Self-Assessment checklist on p. 20 to grade their Unit Assignments. You can also share a copy of the Unit Assignment Rubric (on p. 12 of this Teacher's Handbook) with the students.

Consider the Ideas

A (10 minutes)

1. Direct students to read *The Power Paradox*. Then group students to discuss the title.

2. Elicit students' vocabulary questions. Write the words on the board and provide definitions.

3. Check comprehension. Ask: *What is a paradox? What is the power paradox? What qualities do the best leaders show? How does this article say that power changes people?*

Prepare and Speak

Gather Ideas

A (10 minutes)

1. Direct students to review *The Power Paradox* to find information about how power can affect people.

2. Pair students and have them answer the two questions. Put pairs into larger groups to share their answers.

Organize Ideas

B (15 minutes)

1. Ask a volunteer to read the directions aloud. Preview the chart with students. You may want to model a sample answer. For example, under *Important leadership qualities*, write *Understanding the needs and goals of people*. Individually, have students fill out the chart with their ideas.

2. Circulate around the room, providing help and answering questions as needed.

3. Ask students to share their ideas with a partner. Choose a few volunteers to share their ideas with the class.

Speak

C (20–30 minutes)

1. Go over the directions. Check for understanding by asking: *What are you going to tell us?* (advice for leaders) *What do you need to do during your speech?* (check for understanding)

2. Go over the Self-Assessment checklist with students. Remind them to use vocabulary from the unit if possible. Review the vocabulary if you feel students need a review.

3. Ask students to practice giving their presentations to a partner. Then have students give their presentations to the class. Use the Unit Assignment Rubric on page 12 to evaluate each student's presentation.

Alternative Unit Assignments

Assign or have students choose one of these assignments to do instead of, or in addition to, the Unit Assignment.

1. Do online research about a powerful person who is using his or her power to benefit many people. Tell your classmates about this person in a group presentation.

2. If you were the top official in your school or workplace, what changes would you want to make? How would you go about making those changes? What challenges do you think you would face? Use what you have learned in this unit to prepare a presentation in which you explain some of your ideas and plans.

 For an additional Unit Assignment, have students visit *Q Online Practice*.

Check and Reflect

Check

A (10 minutes)

1. Direct students to read and complete the Self-Assessment checklist.

2. Ask for a show of hands for how many students gave all or mostly *yes* answers.

3. Congratulate them on their success. Discuss the steps they can take if an item on the checklist was difficult for them. For example, if they forgot to check for understanding, encourage them to use this skill regularly in class when they are speaking with their classmates.

Reflect

B (10 minutes)

Ask students to discuss the questions in pairs or small groups. When the conversations have died down, ask: *What new piece of information has stuck with you the most? How did your idea of how power affects leaders change?*

▶ *Listening and Speaking 4, page 21*

Track Your Success (5 minutes)

1. Have students circle the words they have learned in this unit. Suggest that students go back through the unit to review any words they have forgotten.

2. Have students check the skills they have mastered. If students need more practice to feel confident about their proficiency in a skill, point out the page numbers and encourage them to review.

3. Read the learning outcome aloud *(Give a presentation about effective leadership and how to avoid the negative effects of power)*. Ask students if they feel that they have met the outcome.

Unit Assignment Rubric

Student name: _____

Date: _____

Unit Assignment: *Offer advice on how to be an effective leader.*

20 points = Presentation element was completely successful (at least 90% of the time).
15 points = Presentation element was mostly successful (at least 70% of the time).
10 points = Presentation element was partially successful (at least 50% of the time).
 0 points = Presentation element was not successful.

Offer Advice on How to Be an Effective Leader.	20 points	15 points	10 points	0 points
Student spoke clearly and at a good speed about how to be an effective leader.				
Student gave appropriate advice related to the topic of effective leadership.				
Student used vocabulary words from the unit.				
Student used questions or phrases to check for understanding.				
Student used correct syllable stress.				

Total points: _____

Comments:

Unit QUESTION
How does appearance affect our success?

Appearances

LISTENING • identifying details
VOCABULARY • using the dictionary
GRAMMAR • the subjunctive for suggestions
PRONUNCIATION • unstressed syllables
SPEAKING • confirming understanding

LEARNING OUTCOME

Role-play a conversation offering advice to help someone become better organized.

▶ *Listening and Speaking 4, page 23*
Preview the Unit

Learning Outcome

1. Ask a volunteer to read the unit skills and then the unit learning outcome.

2. Explain: *This is what you are expected to be able to do by the unit's end. The learning outcome explains how you are going to be evaluated. With this outcome in mind, you should focus on learning these skills (Listening, Vocabulary, Grammar, Pronunciation, Speaking) that will support your goal of role-playing a conversation offering advice to help someone become better organized. This can also help you act as mentors in the classroom to help the other students meet this outcome.*

A (15 minutes)

1. Write the word *appearance* on the board. Ask students: *What do you think about when you see the word* appearance? *Is appearance important? Why or why not? Does appearance only have to do with how someone looks? What about the appearance of work and living spaces?*

2. Put students in pairs or small groups to discuss the first two questions.

3. Call on volunteers to share their ideas with the class. Ask: *If a person's desk is neat, what do you think about that person? If a person's desk is messy, what do you think about that person? How do you think successful people look?*

4. Focus students' attention on the photo. Have a volunteer describe the photo to the class. Read the third question aloud. Elicit students' answers.

Activity A Answers, p. 23
Answers will vary. Possible answers:
1. My space is messy because I don't have the time to organize it. / My space is neat because I can't do my work if there is clutter around me. / A messy desk says that someone has more important things to do than keep his/her desk neat.
2. Successful people tend to dress well because part of their success is related to what people think of them. People may have negative opinions about someone who looks sloppy.
3. A suit can make someone look successful because people wear suits when they do important jobs.

B (15 minutes)

1. Introduce the Unit Question, *How does appearance affect our success?* Ask related information questions or questions about personal experience to help students prepare for answering the more abstract Unit Question. Say: *Think of successful people you know. How would you describe their appearance? How does your appearance affect what people think about you?*

2. Label four pieces of poster paper with four possible answers to the unit question (e.g., *Messy people are not successful. Organized people are successful. Appearance does not affect success. Messy people can become successful despite their appearance.*) Place each piece of paper in a different corner of the room.

3. Ask students to read and consider the Unit Question for a moment and then to stand in the corner next to the poster that best represents their answer to the question. If students stand by only one or two answers, have them select a second choice to spread the students out a little.

4. Direct the groups in each corner to talk among themselves about the reasons for their answers. Tell them to choose a secretary to record their ideas on the poster paper.

5. Call on volunteers from each corner to share their opinions with the class.

6. Keep the posters for students to refer back to at the end of the unit.

Activity B Answers, p. 23
Answers will vary. Possible answers: If people are messy, other people will not take them seriously. / The neater a person is (or the better dressed), the more successful he or she will become. / In some professions, particularly creative ones, appearance does not affect success as much.

The Q Classroom
 CD1, Track 15

1. Play The Q Classroom. Use the example from the audio to help students continue the conversation. Ask: *How did the students answer the question? Do you agree or disagree with their ideas? Why?*

2. Say: *On the audio, Sophy says that if you dress well, people will think that you're more competent.* Ask: *Why do you think she says this? Does the way that people dress relate to their ability to do their job well?*

▶ Listening and Speaking 4, page 24

C (10 minutes)

1. Ask a volunteer to read the directions, look at the first picture, and give their impression of the first person.

2. Based upon the volunteer's ideas, ask the class how their first impression of this person was affected by her appearance (e.g., *Her jacket shows she may be a businesswoman.*).

3. Have students complete the rest of activity in pairs. Then discuss students' answers to the questions as a class. Have students support their answers.

D (5 minutes)

1. Ask a volunteer to read the directions aloud. Have students check the boxes that reflect their opinions.

2. Pair students to discuss their responses.

3. Discuss any common opinions in the class.

▶ Listening and Speaking 4, page 25

LISTENING

LISTENING 1: A Perfect Mess

VOCABULARY (15 minutes)

1. Direct students to read each sentence and use context clues to guess the meaning of the bold word before they circle the correct definition.

2. Put students in pairs to compare answers. Elicit the answers from volunteers. Read each vocabulary word and have students repeat. Listen for correct syllable stress.

3. Ask questions to help students connect with the vocabulary: *Does an **open-minded** person like new things? What would make your semester **turn out** the way you want it to? Are you the type of person that likes **chaos**? Explain.*

MULTILEVEL OPTION

Pair higher-level students and ask them to write questions, similar to those found in #3 above, using the vocabulary. Then pair lower- and higher-level students and have the higher-level students interview their lower-level partners with the questions.

Vocabulary Answers, pp. 25–26
1. b; **2.** b; **3.** c; **4.** b; **5.** b; **6.** a;
7. a; **8.** c; **9.** c; **10.** c; **11.** c; **12.** a

web For additional practice with the vocabulary, have students visit *Q Online Practice*.

▶ Listening and Speaking 4, page 27

PREVIEW LISTENING 1 (5 minutes)

1. Direct students to read the introduction and complete the activity.

2. Tell students they should review their answer(s) after the listening.

Preview Reading 1 Answer, p. 27
Answers will vary.

Listening 1 Background Note

The listening mentions the scientist Leon Heppel. A child of German immigrants, Heppel picked up an interest in chemistry early in his schooling.

Eventually, he majored in chemistry at University of California, Berkeley, in the United States, and went on to get an advanced degree in biochemistry. Heppel made a number of important discoveries that helped crack the genetic code. Ironically, for a man who had a cluttered desk, he helped organize the genes of the human body.

LISTEN FOR MAIN IDEAS (10 minutes)

 CD1, Track 16

1. Preview the statements with students.

2. Ask students to complete the activity on their own as you play the audio.

3. Ask a volunteer to read each statement. Have students stand up if they believe the answer to be false and remain sitting if they believe the answer to be true. Elicit corrections for the false statements.

> **Listen for Main Ideas Answers, p. 27**
> **1.** T; **2.** F; **3.** F; **4.** T

LISTEN FOR DETAILS (10 minutes)

 CD1, Track 17

1. Have students preview the sentences and answer choices.

2. Play the audio again and have students circle the best answer.

3. Have students compare answers with a partner.

4. Go over the answers with the class.

> **Listen for Details Answers, pp. 27-28**
> **1.** c; **2.** a; **3.** b; **4.** b

 For additional practice with listening comprehension, have students visit *Q Online Practice*.

▶ *Listening and Speaking 4, page 28*

WHAT DO YOU THINK? (15 minutes)

1. Ask students to read the questions and reflect on their answers.

2. Seat students in small groups and assign roles: a group leader to make sure everyone contributes, a note-taker to record the group's ideas, a reporter to share the group's ideas with the class, and a timekeeper to watch the clock.

3. Give students ten minutes to discuss the questions. Call time if conversations are winding down. Allow extra time if necessary.

4. Call on each group's reporter to share ideas with the class.

> **What Do You Think? Answers, p. 28**
> Answers will vary. Possible answers:
> **1.** I'm messy / not messy. I think being messy is a good thing because I can see everything that I need. / I think being messy is not good because you can easily lose things.
> **2.** I think that if a worker's space isn't shared or visible to the public, then the person should be able to be as messy as he or she wants to be.
> **3.** When I was a child, I was not messy at all, and I am still a very neat person. I like to make sure that everything is organized. / When I was a child, I was messy, but now I am neater and more organized.

EXPANSION ACTIVITY:
Round Robin Response (15 minutes)

1. Have each student choose either question 1 or 2 from the What Do You Think activity. Direct them to write five to seven sentences in response, giving their opinion with reasons. Tell them not to write their name at the top.

2. Collect the answers and redistribute them to the class. Have students respond to the answer they have received by agreeing or disagreeing. Collect and redistribute once more and ask students to respond again.

3. After students do this several times, have students return the paper to a pile. Each student should find their original response and read how others responded to them.

Learning Outcome

Use the learning outcome to frame the purpose and relevance of Listening 1. Ask: *What did you learn from Listening 1 that prepares you to role-play a conversation offering advice to help someone become better organized?* (Students learned how being messy may actually be beneficial. They may want to incorporate some of these ideas when they do their role-play.)

Listening Skill: Identifying details
(10 minutes)

1. Go over the information in the skill box.

2. Check comprehension. Ask: *What makes a detail important? What questions should you ask yourself as you listen?*

Skill Note

Listening for details is often hard for language learners, who may capture the main idea of something said but miss the smaller points. Graphic organizers such as charts or webs can help students note details as they listen.

A (10 minutes)

 CD1, Track 18

1. Have a student read the directions aloud. Then preview the chart to ensure students understand how to fill it out.
2. Play the audio and direct students to complete the chart. Replay the audio if students need to hear it again.
3. Have students complete Activity B before going over the information in the chart.

> **Activity A Answers, p. 28**
> Strategies: 1. Put everything in its place. 2. Follow a filing and organization system. 3. Do a little at a time.
> Details:
> Strategy 1: Put everything in a space where it belongs; If it doesn't have a space, make one.
> Strategy 2: Now: Do now; Later: Put in its place; Never: Throw away.
> Strategy 3: Organize step by step; Organize a drawer one day; Organize another thing the next day.

> **MULTILEVEL OPTION**
>
> To support lower-level students, as you play the audio, stop after each strategy is discussed to allow them to complete their notes. Alternatively, play the audio once, and have students first write the strategies in the chart. Then play the audio again, stopping after each section as students fill in the details.

Tip for Success (3 minutes)

1. Read the tip aloud.
2. Remind students that speakers don't often slow down to accommodate note-taking. If students use symbols and abbreviations, they'll be able to write down more information in a shorter amount of time.
3. Provide examples of some helpful abbreviations, such as "w/" for *with*, "w/out" for *without*, "ex" for *example*, and "s/b" and "s/t" for *somebody* and *something*.

▶ *Listening and Speaking 4, page 29*

B (5 minutes)

1. Have students compare their chart with a partner.
2. Elicit the strategies and details from volunteers. You may want to create the chart on the board.
3. Discuss the merits of each detail students chose to write down. Why are they important? How do the details support the main ideas?

For additional practice with listening for details, have students visit *Q Online Practice*.

LISTENING 2:
The Changing Business Dress Code

VOCABULARY (25 minutes)

1. Direct students to read the words and their definitions. Answer any questions about meaning and provide examples of the words in context.
2. Read each word and have students repeat. Listen for correct syllable stress.
3. Ask students to complete the sentences.
4. Call on volunteers to read the sentences aloud.
5. Ask students to choose three words and write a new sentence for each word. Put students in pairs to read their sentences to each other.
6. Ask volunteers to read their sentences aloud.

> **Vocabulary Answers, pp. 29–30**
> **1.** appropriate; **2.** morale; **3.** trend;
> **4.** norm; **5.** investor; **6.** reward;
> **7.** cycle; **8.** anecdote; **9.** associate;
> **10.** conduct; **11.** enthusiasm; **12.** cautious

> **MULTILEVEL OPTION**
>
> For the writing part of the activity, pair lower-level students and have them choose the same three words and write their sentences together. Then group lower-level pairs with other pairs to share their sentences.

 For additional practice with the vocabulary, have students visit *Q Online Practice*.

▶ *Listening and Speaking 4, page 30*

Tip for Success (1 minute)

1. Read the tip aloud.

2. Ask students what strategies they use to remember new words. Suggest that they include pictures or example sentences on the flashcards they make for new words.

PREVIEW LISTENING 2 (5 minutes)

1. Read the introduction aloud.

2. Place students into mixed-ability pairs and have them discuss the questions.

3. Tell students they should review their answer(s) after the listening.

Listening 2 Background Note

In many countries, the formality of business dress often varies from industry to industry, regardless of trends. In the finance and law industries, for example, business dress is very formal. Other industries, especially those considered more creative, have a more casual dress code that may allow employees to express their creativity.

Teaching Note

Students may find these words and phrases difficult:

ditch: (v) *to get rid of something or someone because you no longer want or need it/them*

turn(ed) up: (phr v) *to arrive*

▶ *Listening and Speaking 4, page 31*
LISTEN FOR MAIN IDEAS (10 minutes)

🔊 CD1, Track 19

1. Read the directions. Allow students time to preview the questions.

2. Ask students to complete the activity individually as you play the audio.

3. Ask volunteers to share their answers. Encourage them to provide evidence from the listening to support their answers.

> **Listen for Main Ideas Answers, p. 31**
> **1.** b; **2.** a; **3.** b; **4.** c

LISTEN FOR DETAILS (10 minutes)

🔊 CD1, Track 20

1. Direct students to read the questions. Remind students of the listening for details skills practice they did earlier in the unit.

2. Play the audio again as students take notes. Replay the audio if necessary. Then have students use their notes to answer the questions.

3. Have students compare answers with a partner.

4. Go over the answers with the class.

> **Listen for Details Answers, p. 31**
> Answers may vary. Possible answers:
> **1.** Executives thought casual dress would increase productivity.
> **2.** Investors are more cautious about casually dressed business executives now because they think formal wear reflects a more professional attitude and that casual wear reflects a less professional attitude.
> **3.** Casual or sloppy dress is sometimes associated with a less professional or careless attitude.
> **4.** Now it is important to younger workers to dress very professionally at work.

 For additional practice with listening for details, have students visit *Q Online Practice*.

▶ *Listening and Speaking 4, page 32*
WHAT DO YOU THINK?

A (15 minutes)

1. Ask students to read the questions and reflect on their answers.

2. Seat students in small groups and assign roles: a group leader to make sure everyone contributes, a note-taker to record the group's ideas, a reporter to share the group's ideas with the class, and a timekeeper to watch the clock.

3. Give students ten minutes to discuss the questions. Call time if conversations are winding down. Allow extra time if necessary.

4. Have each group's reporter share their group's answers with the class.

> **Activity A Answers, p. 32**
> Answers will vary. Possible answers:
> **1.** If an employee did his or her job extremely well, that person's appearance wouldn't impact my decision about a promotion. / People who want to be promoted need to dress neatly. If they didn't, I wouldn't promote them.
> **2.** I liked wearing a uniform to school because we weren't judged on what we were wearing. / A disadvantage of wearing a uniform is that people can't express who they are as easily.

B (10 minutes)

1. Tell the students that they should think about both Listening 1 and Listening 2 as they answer the questions in Activity B.

2. Call on groups to share their ideas with the class.

> **Activity B Answers, p. 32**
> Answers will vary. Possible answers:
> **1.** First impressions are very important, and if someone is or isn't organized, I might make judgments about his or her personality.
> **2.** Often my first impression has been wrong. I learned that messy people can be good at their jobs.

Learning Outcome

Use the learning outcome to frame the purpose and relevance of Listenings 1 and 2. Ask: *What did you learn from Listenings 1 and 2 that prepares you to role-play a conversation offering advice to help someone become better organized?* (Students learned about the effects and consequences of being messy and dressing formally/informally. These ideas may help them when they present their role-plays.)

Vocabulary Skill: Using the dictionary
(15 minutes)

1. Ask a volunteer to read the information about using the dictionary. Remind students of the lesson from Unit 1 about finding the meaning of words from context.

2. Check comprehension: *What can you do to choose the correct definition of a word?* (consider the context; determine part of speech)

3. Read the example sentence. Use the dictionary entry to model how to select the correct definition of the word *fade*.

Skill Note

Often the same word can be several parts of speech. *Green,* for example, can be a noun (slang for money; an area of grass), a verb (to become environmentally friendly), and an adjective (the color). Figuring out the part of speech of a word helps students efficiently sort through definitions in the dictionary and select the correct one for the context. Online linguistic corpora and learner's dictionaries give teachers and students examples of how the same word is used as a

noun, verb, or adjective. Type in one word, like *green,* into an online linguistic corpus, and you will receive hundreds of examples of that word in real sentences.

▶ *Listening and Speaking 4, page 33*

A (5 minutes)

1. Direct students to work with a partner to complete the activity.

2. Go over the answers with the class.

> **Activity A Answers, p. 33**
> **1.** to get rid of something or someone because you no longer want or need it/ them
> **2.** without emotion; unfriendly

B (15 minutes)

1. Direct students to work on their own to discover and write the definitions of the words. Have them check their answers with a partner.

2. Check answers as a class. Ask students to identify the part of speech of each bold word.

> **Activity B Answers, p. 33**
> **1.** serious
> **2.** a sum of money that you have to pay for breaking a law or rule
> **3.** an event, an action, a fact, etc., that shows that something exists, is happening, or may happen in the future
> **4.** to put clothes on someone or yourself

 For additional practice with using the dictionary, have students visit *Q Online Practice.*

21ST CENTURY SKILLS

Using a dictionary to find the right definition of a word often requires good analytical skills. Analysis, which is the ability to look at information with a critical eye, is a key skill students need to develop. As students progress in their education and advance in the workplace, they will need to look at more and more information, analyze its usefulness, and figure out what to do with it. The more efficient students can be at selecting information that can be useful to them, the quicker they will be able to do what they are required to do in a given situation.

SPEAKING

Grammar: The subjunctive for suggestions (15 minutes)

1. In advance of discussing the subjunctive for suggestions, write these two grammatical structures on the board:
   1. suggesting verb + indirect object (IO) + base form of verb
   2. suggesting expression + indirect object (IO) + base form of verb

2. Ask three higher-level students to read the information and examples in the book, splitting the length of the reading between them. Pause to answer questions, clarify, or provide additional examples.

3. Check comprehension: *Why do we use the subjunctive? Does the subjunctive form change depending on the person you are talking about? Does the subjunctive form change when you are using the past tense?*

4. Refer students to the patterns on the board. Elicit some example sentences with the subjunctive using some of the verbs or expressions from the chart.

A (10 minutes)

1. Read the directions aloud and do the first sentence together as a class.

2. Direct students to complete the activity individually.

3. When finished, students should check their answers with a partner.

4. Go over the answers as a class.

> **Activity A Answers, p. 35**
> **1.** Customers demand that sales reps dress more formally.
> **2.** It is recommended that employees avoid looking sloppy at work.
> **3.** When posing for a work-related picture, it's a good idea that CEOs not wear shorts and sandals.
> **4.** Some executives advise that employees ditch their casual clothes.
> **5.** Some experts suggest that managers offer a "dress-up Monday" option.
> **6.** It's a good idea that people dress more formally at work.

B (10 minutes)

1. Read the directions aloud. Direct students to write suggestions using the subjunctive. Refer them to page 34 for help.

2. When finished, have students share their suggestions with a partner.

3. Ask volunteers to share their sentences with the class.

> **Activity B Answers, pp. 35–36**
> Answers will vary. Possible answers:
> Picture A:
> **1.** I recommend that he buy a suit.
> **2.** It's important that he dress more formally.
> Picture B:
> **1.** I suggest that she wear more business casual clothing.
> **2.** I recommend that she not wear a suit to work.

 For additional practice with using the subjunctive for suggestions, have students visit *Q Online Practice*.

Pronunciation: Unstressed syllables (10 minutes)

CD1, Track 21

1. Read the first paragraph in the skill box. Then play the audio. Ask for volunteers to read the sample word *appearances*. Correct pronunciation as needed.

2. Go over the remainder of the instruction in the box. Allow students to practice making the /ə/ sound.

3. Check comprehension by asking questions: *What happens to vowels in unstressed syllables? How do you make the unstressed "schwa" sound? Which kinds of vowels are long and clear?*

Skill Note

Not only is the *schwa* the most common vowel sound in English, it is *the most common* sound in English overall. Getting the *schwa* correct is a matter of relaxing one's mouth—dropping one's jaw and lowering one's tongue—and then releasing a sound from the back of one's throat. The tendency is to hold the sound for a long time to understand how it sounds, but in practice, this unstressed vowel sound is very short—which can make it hard for students to hear it in everyday speech.

A (10 minutes)

CD1, Track 22

1. Review the directions with the class.

2. Before playing the audio, have students pronounce the words in pairs. Ask them to try to guess where the unstressed syllables are by listening for the schwa sound. Avoid providing answers; they'll find the answers in the audio.

3. Play the audio. Have students underline the unstressed syllables individually. When complete, students should review answers with a partner.

4. Elicit and confirm answers as a class.

> **Activity A Answers, p. 36**
> **1.** pleasure;   **2.** forgotten;
> **3.** successful;   **4.** habit;
> **5.** business;   **6.** allow;
> **7.** cautious;   **8.** professional

Tip for Success (1 minute)

1. Read the tip aloud.

2. Ask students about their experiences with online dictionaries. Ask: *Do you use the pronunciation audio when you use online dictionaries?* Encourage students to use these audio pronunciation features within online dictionaries and to repeat what they hear.

B (5 minutes)

CD1, Track 23

Have students listen again and repeat the words.

▶ *Listening and Speaking 4, page 37*

Critical Thinking Tip (1 minute)

1. Ask a volunteer to read the tip aloud.

2. Explain that restating what the speaker has said shows that you are listening and gives both of you a chance to identify any misunderstandings and clear them up.

Critical Q: Expansion Activity

Restate

Place students into pairs and have them answer the following question: *Why do some people want to change their appearance?*

As each student talks, have their partners take notes about their ideas. After one student is finished speaking, have the other use their notes to restate their partners' opinions.

Repeat the activity with another question, but this time, don't have students take notes. Have them restate by remembering what their partners said.

Speaking Skill: Confirming understanding (15 minutes)

1. Check for previous knowledge. Ask: *What phrases do you use to make sure you understand what someone else is saying?* Write some of these phrases on the board.

2. Go over the information and examples in the skill box.

3. Check comprehension by asking questions: *What phrases can you use to make sure you understand what someone is saying? What words or phrases can you use to signal that you now understand the information?*

4. Pair students and have them practice saying the new phrases to each other.

A (10 minutes)

CD1, Track 24

1. Have a volunteer read the directions aloud.

2. Play the audio. Have students complete each conversation.

3. Go over the answers with the class.

4. Then have partners practice the conversations.

> **Activity A Answers, pp. 37–38**
> **1.** So you mean that
> **2.** Are you saying; Got it
> **3.** If I understand you; OK
> **4.** Does that mean; I see

▶ *Listening and Speaking 4, page 38*

B (20 minutes)

1. Put students into groups to discuss each question. Remind them to use the questions and phrases from the Speaking Skill box on page 37.

2. You may want to have a volunteer from each group serve as a "monitor" to make sure that everyone checks for understanding during the discussion of each question.

> **Activity B Answers, p. 38**
> Answers will vary. Possible answers:
> **1.** If people look sloppy, they may be sloppy with their work too.

2. It doesn't matter because the most important thing is that people have the skills to do their job. However, if they have to meet with clients, their clothing and workspace should probably look neat.
3. Organization leads to success, so I think that schools should teach students to be organized.

Tip for Success (1 minute)

1. Read the tip aloud.
2. Remind students that it takes two people to participate in a conversation. Confirming understanding with short words or phrases is a way to let your conversation partner know that you are listening to what they are saying.

 For additional practice with confirming understanding, have students visit *Q Online Practice*.

Unit Assignment: Role-play

Unit Question (5 minutes)

Refer students back to the ideas they discussed at the beginning of the unit about how appearance might affect success. Cue students if necessary by asking specific questions about the content of the unit: *In our discussions, how did we decide that appearance might affect success? Does it affect success at all? Does being messy sometimes help people be successful?* Read the direction lines for the assignment together to ensure understanding.

Learning Outcome

1. Tie the Unit Assignment to the unit learning outcome. Say: *The outcome for this unit is to role-play a conversation offering advice to help someone become better organized. This Unit Assignment is going to let you show your skill in giving advice as well as confirming understanding, pronouncing unstressed syllables, and using the subjunctive.*
2. Explain that you are going to use a rubric similar to their Self-Assessment checklist on p. 40 to grade their Unit Assignment. You can also share a copy of the Unit Assignment Rubric (on p. 23 of this *Teacher's Handbook*) with the students.
3. Note that each student will be evaluated individually even though they will do the role-play in pairs.
4. If appropriate, have students use the rubric to grade each other as they perform their role-plays.

Consider the Ideas (15 minutes)

1. Place students into groups of three and direct them to brainstorm situations at school or work that can create a mess. Then have students discuss how they can make those situations better.
2. Place two groups together and have them share their ideas and solutions. Encourage students to add to each other's ideas.
3. Elicit ideas from the class and note them on the board.

▶ *Listening and Speaking 4, page 39*

Prepare and Speak

Gather Ideas

A (10 minutes)

1. Direct students to read the information about the client and take notes about his situation in the chart provided.
2. Pair students and have them compare their notes. Put pairs into larger groups to share ideas.

▶ *Listening and Speaking 4, page 40*

Organize Ideas

B (15 minutes)

1. Ask a volunteer to read the directions aloud.
2. Preview the chart with students and have them complete it individually.
3. Elicit advice from the class.

Speak

C (30–45 minutes)

1. Go over the instructions. Check for understanding by asking: *What kind of language should the advice giver use? What kind of language should Dan Howard use?* Refer students to the grammar and speaking skill boxes on pages 34 and 37.
2. Have students practice the role-plays in pairs. Then have them present their role-play to the class. Use the Unit Assignment Rubric on page 23 to evaluate each student.
3. Alternatively, have students present their role-play to another pair and score each other using the rubric.

Alternative Unit Assignments

Assign or have students choose one of these assignments to do instead of, or in addition to, the Unit Assignment.

1. Present this question to the class: *How would you feel about these people? 1. a doctor in jeans and a T-shirt 2. a famous athlete in a business suit.* Place students into pairs for a role-play and have one be the person named and have the other be a person who is commenting on their appearance.

2. Companies vary in their dress codes and their expectations when it comes to appearance. Make a list of jobs you might like to have in the future. How might your appearance have to change if you took a job in one of these professions? Do online research of a profession you are interested in. Find out about the dress-code expectations for that profession.

 For an additional Unit Assignment, have students visit *Q Online Practice*.

Check and Reflect

Check

A (10 minutes)

1. Direct students to read and complete the Self-Assessment checklist.

2. Ask for a show of hands for how many students gave all or mostly *yes* answers.

3. Congratulate them on their success. Discuss the steps they can take if an item on the checklist was difficult for them. For example, if they didn't use questions or phrases to confirm understanding, encourage students to do this more regularly when they have discussions with each other in class.

Reflect

B (10 minutes)

Ask students to consider the questions in pairs. When the conversations have died down, have students share something new that they have learned. Ask: *How have your ideas about appearance and success changed?*

▶ *Listening and Speaking 4, page 41*

Track Your Success (5 minutes)

1. Have students circle the words they have learned in this unit. Suggest that students go back through the unit to review any words they have forgotten.

2. Have students check the skills they have mastered. If students need more practice to feel confident about their proficiency in a skill, point out the page numbers and encourage them to review.

3. Read the learning outcome aloud *(Role-play a conversation offering advice to help someone become better organized)*. Ask students if they feel that they have met the outcome.

Unit Assignment Rubric

Student name: _____

Date: _____

Unit Assignment: *Role-play a conversation.*

20 points = Speaking element was completely successful (at least 90% of the time).
15 points = Speaking element was mostly successful (at least 70% of the time).
10 points = Speaking element was partially successful (at least 50% of the time).
 0 points = Speaking element was not successful.

Role-play a conversation	20 points	15 points	10 points	0 points
Student spoke easily and clearly about how to help someone become better organized.				
Student supported his or her opinion with clear examples.				
Student used the subjunctive when giving advice.				
Student confirmed understanding of what their role-play partner said at least twice.				
Student pronounced unstressed syllables correctly.				

Total points: _____

Comments:

Unit QUESTION

When does a child become an adult?

Growing Up

LISTENING • making predictions
VOCABULARY • using the dictionary
GRAMMAR • phrasal verbs
PRONUNCIATION • sentence stress patterns
SPEAKING • giving a presentation

LEARNING OUTCOME

Present a personal story describing an important event in your life that made you feel like an adult.

▶ *Listening and Speaking 4, page 43*

Preview the Unit

Learning Outcome

1. Ask a volunteer to read the unit skills and then the unit learning outcome.

2. Explain: *This is what you are expected to be able to do by the unit's end. The learning outcome explains how you are going to be evaluated. With this outcome in mind, you should focus on learning these skills (Listening, Vocabulary, Grammar, Pronunciation, Speaking) that will support your goal of presenting a story describing an important event in your life that made you feel like an adult. This can also help you act as mentors in the classroom to help the other students meet this outcome.*

A (15 minutes)

1. To get students thinking about adulthood, ask: *At what age did you consider yourself an adult? What life events make people feel like adults?* Provide some examples from your life that relate to becoming an adult.

2. Put students in pairs or small groups to discuss the first two questions.

3. Call on volunteers to share their ideas with the class. Ask: *At what age did you become an adult? Is this the age that all children become adults? Why or why not?*

4. Focus students' attention on the photo. Have a volunteer describe the photo to the class. Read the third question aloud. Elicit students' answers.

Activity A Answers, p. 43
Answers will vary. Possible answers:
1. I became an adult at 18 because that is when I moved out of my parents' house.

2. Getting married or starting work can make someone feel like an adult.
3. The boy is happy because he gets to do what his father is doing.

B (15 minutes)

1. Introduce the Unit Question, *When does a child become an adult?* Ask related information questions or questions about personal experience to help students prepare for answering the more abstract Unit Question. Ask: *What does it mean to be a child? What does it mean to be an adult?*

2. Read the Unit Question aloud. Point out that answers to the Unit Question can fall into categories (e.g., at a particular age, when a person has professional responsibilities, when a person has personal responsibilities). Give students a minute to silently consider their answers to the question.

3. Write each category at the top of a sheet of poster paper. Elicit answers to the Unit Question and make notes of the answers under the correct category. Post the lists to refer to later in the unit.

Activity B Answers, p. 43
Answers will vary. Possible answers: A child becomes an adult at age 18. / A child becomes an adult when he or she can live on their own. / A child becomes an adult when he or she gets married.

The Q Classroom
CD1, Track 25

1. Play The Q Classroom. Use the example from the audio to help students continue the conversation. Ask: *How did the students answer the question? Do you agree or disagree with their ideas? Why?*

2. Ask students to add any answers from the audio to the lists from Activity B.

C (10 minutes)

1. Review the experiences on the list as a class.

2. Have students individually check their top three choices. Then pair students to share their answers.

3. Group pairs into larger groups to share their answers once more. Have students focus on the experiences they all chose, if there are any. Ask: *Why do you think you all chose this experience?* Alternatively, if one experience was not chosen by anyone in the group, ask: *Why do you think no one chose this experience?*

Activity C Answers, p. 44
Answers will vary.

MULTILEVEL OPTION

Have lower-level students draw a picture of a typical child or a typical adult. Have higher-level students interview the lower-level students (in pairs) about why they chose to draw the picture the way that they did.

D (15 minutes)

1. Pair students and have them read the statements. Direct them to discuss whether they agree or disagree with the statements. Remind students to support their opinions with details.

2. Once the students have discussed each statement, have the class vote on their favorite statements.

3. Ask a volunteer to write the top two or three choices on the board. Discuss the meaning of those statements as a class.

Expansion Activity: Share Proverbs (15 minutes)

1. Every culture has proverbs or sayings about age. Ask students to think of proverbs about age from their culture. Allow students to write the proverbs in their home languages if they need to.

2. Put students in pairs or small groups to share the proverbs or sayings and discuss what they mean. Group students from different countries if possible.

3. Call on volunteers to share their proverbs with the class.

LISTENING

LISTENING 1: Generation Next

VOCABULARY (10 minutes)

1. Direct students to read the vocabulary words and definitions. Answer any questions about meaning and provide examples of the words in context.

2. Pronounce each word and have students repeat. Listen for correct syllable stress.

3. Then have students complete each sentence with the correct vocabulary word.

4. Call on volunteers to read the sentences aloud.

Vocabulary Answers, pp. 45–46
1. initiation;	**2.** run;	**3.** marker;
4. contradiction;	**5.** morally;	**6.** entitled;
7. contributor;	**8.** assume;	**9.** carefree;
10. milestones;	**11.** transition;	**12.** pinpoint

 For additional practice with the vocabulary, have students visit *Q Online Practice*.

PREVIEW LISTENING 1 (10 minutes)

1. Have a volunteer read the introduction and question aloud.

2. Instruct students to select an answer and share the reason for their selection with a partner. Poll the class to see how many students selected each age.

3. Tell students they should review their answer after the listening.

Preview Listening 1 Answer, p. 46
Answers will vary.

Listening 1 Background Note

Dr. Cynthia Lightfoot is a professor of human development and family studies at Penn State Brandywine, in Pennsylvania. She is primarily concerned with the development of children. Some of the titles of books she's written or co-written include *The Development of Children* and *The Culture of Adolescent Risk-Taking*. She says that her own experiences have made her interested in studying children in family relationships.

LISTEN FOR MAIN IDEAS (10 minutes)

 CD1, Track 26

1. Ask students to preview the statements.

2. Play the audio. Have students complete the activity individually.

3. Check answers as a class. Elicit corrections for the false statements.

> **Listen for Main Ideas Answers, p. 46**
> **1.** F; **2.** T; **3.** T; **4.** F; **5.** T

▶ *Listening and Speaking 4, page 47*

LISTEN FOR DETAILS (10 minutes)

 CD1, Track 27

1. Read the directions aloud and have students preview the questions and answer choices.

2. Play the audio and direct students to circle the correct answers.

3. Have students compare answers with a partner. Go over the answers with the class.

> **Listen for Details Answers, p. 47**
> **1.** a; **2.** c; **3.** b; **4.** b; **5.** a

For additional practice with listening comprehension, have students visit *Q Online Practice*.

WHAT DO YOU THINK? (15 minutes)

1. Ask students to read the questions and reflect on their answers.

2. Seat students in small groups and assign roles: a group leader to make sure everyone contributes, a note-taker to record the group's ideas, a reporter to share the group's ideas with the class, and a timekeeper to watch the clock.

3. Give students ten minutes to discuss the questions. Call time if conversations are winding down. Allow them an extra minute or two if necessary.

4. Call on each group's reporter to share ideas with the class.

> **What Do You Think? Answers, p. 47**
> Answers will vary. Possible answers:
> **1.** Traveling helped me grow up. I had to travel to a big city by myself. Being in such a big city without anyone else to rely on helped me learn how to take responsibility for myself.

2. I think that the UN's age of adulthood is too high. People become adults much earlier than 18. / I agree with the UN's age of adulthood. Children aren't ready to make decisions until they are 18.

3. I think there should be some sort of ceremony to mark the transition from childhood to adulthood because it gives children something to look forward to. / I don't think there needs to be an initiation into adulthood. People will become adults when they're ready.

Learning Outcome

Use the learning outcome to frame the purpose and relevance of Listening 1. Ask: *What did you learn from Listening 1 that prepares you to present a story describing an important event in your life that made you feel like an adult?* (Students learned how different societies view the act of becoming an adult. They may want to refer to these ideas when they give their presentations.)

▶ *Listening and Speaking 4, page 48*

Listening Skill: Making predictions
(10 minutes)

1. Ask a student to read the information about making predictions. Check comprehension: *What is a prediction? What information do you use to make a prediction?*

2. Discuss with students when it is useful to make predictions in class.

Critical Thinking Tip (1 minute)

1. Read the Critical Thinking Tip aloud.

2. Ask students when they have used predicting in the past to help understand material in English or in their native language.

Critical Q: Expansion Activity

Predict

Bring in several pictures of people or places that are large enough to be seen by all of the members of the class at once.

Tell students to make predictions about the pictures. Hold each picture up in turn and ask: *What do you think this person's life is like?* (if the picture is of a person). Or ask: *What do you think happens here?* (if the picture is of a place).

Ask students to think about their own experiences and use visual clues in the pictures to make predictions. Elicit predictions from volunteers. If you know the actual circumstances surrounding those people or places, tell them to students so they can assess if their predictions were correct.

A (10 minutes)

1. Ask a student to read the directions aloud. Have students complete the activity individually.

2. Direct students to share their ideas with a partner.

3. Elicit ideas from volunteers.

> **Activity A Answers, pp. 48–49**
> Answers will vary.

Tip for Success (5 minutes)

1. Ask a volunteer to read the tip aloud.

2. Show students an example of a word web. Tell students that graphic organizers are useful because they help people organize their ideas.

▶ *Listening and Speaking 4, page 49*

B (15 minutes)

CD1, Track 28

1. Ask a volunteer to read the directions aloud. Have students preview the questions and answers.

2. Play the audio and direct students to complete the activity individually.

3. Have students review their answers in small groups. Elicit the answers from volunteers. Ask: *What clues did you hear that made you choose your answer?*

> **Activity B Answers, p. 49**
> **1.** a; **2.** c; **3.** a; **4.** c

 For additional practice with making predictions, have students visit *Q Online Practice.*

▶ *Listening and Speaking 4, page 50*

LISTENING 2: Growing Up Quickly

VOCABULARY (25 minutes)

1. Read the directions. Read sentence 1 together. Elicit guesses from students about what *sibling* means. Point out any context clues. Then find the correct definition.

2. Put students into groups to complete the activity. Remind them to try to guess the meaning of each bold word first, before finding the definition.

3. Check answers as a class. Then choose a few words and have pairs create one new sentence for each word.

4. Ask volunteers to write their sentences on the board. Correct as a class if necessary.

> **Vocabulary Answers, pp. 50–51**
> **a.** in charge of;   **b.** burden;   **c.** frustration;
> **d.** confusion;   **e.** sibling;   **f.** reverse;
> **g.** resent;   **h.** satisfaction;   **i.** capable;
> **j.** isolation;   **k.** barrier;   **l.** guidance

MULTILEVEL OPTION

Pair lower- and higher-level students to write the additional sample sentences.

 For additional practice with the vocabulary, have students visit *Q Online Practice.*

▶ *Listening and Speaking 4, page 51*

PREVIEW LISTENING 2 (10 minutes)

1. Read the introduction and have students complete the task individually. Then have them share their answers with a partner.

2. Ask: *Which emotions do you think children with adult responsibilities feel? Why? Which emotion did most of you choose? Why was this emotion a popular choice?*

3. Tell students to review their answers after listening.

> **Preview Listening 2 Answers, p. 51**
> Answers will vary.

Listening 2 Background Note

Share this note with students *after* Listening 2. As a young child, President Clinton was left with his grandparents while his mother studied nursing. This early experience with his grandparents had a lasting impact on the future president of the United States. Research shows that events in a child's early years may resonate throughout the rest of his or her life. Also, children retain information from their adolescence that they may analyze and make use of when they get older.

LISTEN FOR MAIN IDEAS (10 minutes)

🔊 CD1, Track 29

1. Read the directions. Ask volunteers to read the sentences.

2. Play the audio and have students work individually to check their ideas.

3. After listening, have students compare their answers with one another. Replay the audio if needed.

4. Check answers as a class. Ask: *What clues in the audio helped you choose your answers?*

Listen for Main Ideas Answers, p. 51
Checked: Too much responsibility can be a burden on children. / Children often have to take on the role of parent to care for siblings. / Some children even reverse roles with their own parents. / Responsibilities can be barriers and cause frustration. / Many of these children become teachers and counselors.

▶ *Listening and Speaking 4, page 52*

LISTEN FOR DETAILS (10 minutes)

🔊 CD1, Track 30

1. Direct students to preview the statements and listen again to the lecture, marking their answers as they listen.

2. Read the statements aloud. Have students raise their left hands for *false* and their right hands for *true*. Elicit corrections for the false statements.

Listen for Details Answers, p. 51
1. F; **2.** T; **3.** F; **4.** T; **5.** F; **6.** F; **7.** T; **8.** T

 For additional practice with listening comprehension, have students visit *Q Online Practice*.

❓ WHAT DO YOU THINK?

A (15 minutes)

1. Ask students to read the questions and reflect on their answers.

2. Seat students in small groups and assign roles: a group leader to make sure everyone contributes, a note-taker to record the group's ideas, a reporter to share the group's ideas with the class, and a timekeeper to watch the clock.

3. Give students ten minutes to discuss the questions. Call time if conversations are winding down. Allow them an extra minute or two if necessary.

4. Call on each group's reporter to share ideas with the class.

Activity A Answers, p. 52
Answers will vary. Possible answers:
1. I had a lot of responsibilities as a child. I had to make dinner every night, pack lunch for my brother every morning, and find time to do all of my homework.
2. I think some adult responsibility is good for a child, but too much is bad. Kids should have the chance to be kids.

B (10 minutes)

1. Tell the students that they should think about both Listening 1 and Listening 2 as they answer the questions in Activity B.

2. Call on each group to share ideas with the class.

Activity B Answers, p. 52
Answers will vary. Possible answers:
1. If children have to act like parents to their brothers and sisters or take care of their parents who are sick, then they will definitely grow up faster. Other family members, like an aunt, uncle, or grandparent, can help children in these situations. Perhaps a health-care worker could help a parent who is very ill, which would take some of the burden off of the child.
2. I think life events really determine the transition from childhood to adulthood. When you get married or move into your own home, you are making a decision to be more independent and take on adult responsibilities.

Learning Outcome

Use the learning outcome to frame the purpose and relevance of Listenings 1 and 2. Ask: *What did you learn from Listenings 1 and 2 that prepares you to present a story describing an important event in your life that made you feel like an adult?* (Students learned about different experiences children have that can make them feel like an adult. These ideas may help them when they give their presentations.)

▶ *Listening and Speaking 4, page 53*

Vocabulary Skill: Using the dictionary
(10 minutes)

1. Present the information on using the dictionary and ask volunteers to read the dictionary definitions aloud.

2. Ask students to think of other pairs of words that are similar but don't mean exactly the same thing (e.g., *parent / adult; money / cash*).

Language patterns can help students determine how vocabulary words are used in sentences. Students can find these patterns in the entries of a learner's dictionary. For example, the word *demonstrate* is never followed by an object pronoun (like *me*). You demonstrate something (~sth) to somebody (to sb). So it's clear that in Activity A number 3, *show* is the word that must be used with *us*.

A (10 minutes)

1. Ask a volunteer to read the definitions in number 1. Elicit from the class any differences they see between the two words. Ask students to write the words in the blanks.

2. Direct students to complete the activity.

3. Go over the answers with the class.

> **Activity A Answers, pp. 53–54**
> **1a.** financial;   **1b.** economic;
> **2a.** ceremony;   **2b.** rite;
> **3a.** demonstrate;   **3b.** show

Cultural Note

Activity A mentions fraternities. Fraternities are groups for men on college campuses that encourage brotherhood, friendship, and academic success. Men take part in activities in order to join these groups, and if accepted, they live together, work in their communities, and watch out for each other. Women can join similar groups called sororities.

EXPANSION ACTIVITY: Using an Online Corpus
(10 minutes)

1. If you have Internet access in your classroom, find an online corpus (search "Corpus" in an Internet search engine).

2. Have students search the six vocabulary words from Activity A. When the example sentences are called up, have students notice which words are used *around* the vocabulary words.

3. When students are learning new vocabulary words, encourage them to note how they are used in sentences.

▶ *Listening and Speaking 4, page 54*

B (20 minutes)

1. Ask students to look up the words in a dictionary and write original sentences. Then have students read their sentences to a partner. Circulate around

the room to ensure that students are using the correct definitions of the words.

2. Ask volunteers to write their sentences on the board. Correct the sentences as necessary.

> **Activity B Answers, p. 54**
> Answers will vary.

MULTILEVEL OPTION

Have lower-level students work in pairs to look up the words and write their sentences together.

 For additional practice with words with similar meanings, have students visit *Q Online Practice.*

▶ *Listening and Speaking 4, page 55*

SPEAKING

Grammar: Phrasal verbs (15 minutes)

1. Ask volunteers to read the sections one by one. Provide additional explanations or examples as needed.

2. Ask: *What phrasal verbs do you already know? What two words create a phrasal verb? What does a particle look like?*

3. Check comprehension: *What's the difference between a transitive and an intransitive verb?* Ask volunteers to provide an example of a sentence with a transitive phrasal verb and an intransitive phrasal verb.

Tip for Success (1 minute)

1. Ask a volunteer to read the tip aloud.

2. Encourge students to use all of the information listed under a given word in the dictionary. Make sure students also pay special attention to example sentences because they can help them learn how to use a new word.

Skill Note

Phrasal verbs are unique to Germanic languages, such as English. There are thousands of phrasal verbs in English, and they are often used in informal speech. Therefore, it is critical that students learn phrasal verbs and what they mean in order to participate in conversations with native speakers. You may want to highlight the difference between a verb + a preposition vs. a phrasal verb that includes the same two words. For example, in the sentence *He looked up at the sky*, the verb and preposition *looked up* has a literal meaning. In the sentence *He looked up the word in the dictionary*, the phrasal verb *looked up* has an idiomatic meaning. It is this idiomatic or figurative meaning that makes phrasal verbs unique and important.

▶ *Listening and Speaking 4, page 56*

A (15 minutes)

CD1, Track 31

1. Have a student read the directions aloud. Ask: *What's the missing word in each phrasal verb?* (a particle)

2. Play the audio. Have students complete the phrasal verbs individually.

3. Go over the answers with the class.

> **Activity A Answers, p. 56**
> **1.** on; **2.** up; **3.** away; **4.** into; **5.** up; **6.** in

B (10 minutes)

1. Ask a volunteer to read the directions. Review the difference between transitive and intransitive phrasal verbs.

2. Have students complete the activity alone or in pairs. Monitor pairs to verify answers.

3. Elicit the answers from volunteers.

> **Activity B Answers, p. 56**
> **1.** work out; T;   **2.** got on; I;   **3.** go on; I;
> **4.** giving up; T;   **5.** take care of; T;   **6.** get out of; I

 For additional practice with phrasal verbs, have students visit *Q Online Practice*.

Pronunciation: Sentence stress (15 minutes)

CD1, Track 32

1. Read the information on sentence stress.

2. Check comprehension. Ask: *When you say a sentence, which words do you stress? What's a content word? What's a function word?*

3. Go over the chart on page 57. Write some sentences on the board (*e.g., I live in Toronto. He wore a blue shirt. Do you like pizza?*). Ask students which words in these sentences might be stressed. Discuss the difference between content words and function words.

4. Play the audio with the example sentence. Ask students to practice the sentence, stressing the underlined words.

▶ *Listening and Speaking 4, page 57*

A (10 minutes)

CD1, Track 33

1. Direct students to underline the stressed words as they listen to the sentences on the audio track.

2. Put students in pairs to compare answers and practice reading the sentences with the correct stress.

3. Call on volunteers to identify the stressed words and read the sentences to the class.

> **Activity A Answers, p. 57**
> **1.** become, employed, call, adult
> **2.** how, much, provide, yourself
> **3.** I, married
> **4.** become, adult, 16
> **5.** day, adult, day, do, whatever, want, do
> **6.** age, become, adult, varies

Skill Note

Sometimes a speaker will stress a function word in order to emphasize something specific in his or her message. For example, the speaker of sentence 3 in Activity A stresses the word *I* at the beginning of the sentence in order to emphasize that this is a personal opinion.

B (15 minutes)

1. Direct students to read the conversation and underline the content words. Remind them to refer to the chart of content words and function words at the top of the page.

2. In pairs, students should read the conversation aloud and practice placing correct stress on the content words.

> **Activity B Answers, p. 57**
> Happy, Birthday; Thanks, can't, believe, already, 18 years old; yeah, adult, now, don't, feel, adult, kid; really, taking, care, younger, siblings, years, now, feel, pretty, grown up, still, live, home, still, rely, parents, a lot; maybe, change, now, 18

 For additional practice with sentence stress, have students visit *Q Online Practice*.

Part of growing up and becoming a successful member of academic and workplace teams is realizing that failure can be an opportunity to learn. Google, Facebook, and Apple did not become successful without first failing. Each company had (and continues to have) setbacks with new products, services, and customer service. With each less-than-successful experience, these companies learn how to be better at what they do. Innovation aims for eventual success while assuming short-term failure. In academic and work life, it might be useful to approach projects and tasks with the same attitude. Failure can lead to success if you're learning along the way.

▶ *Listening and Speaking 4, page 58*

Speaking Skill: Giving a presentation
(15 minutes)

1. Probe for previous knowledge. Ask: *Have you ever given a presentation? How do you prepare for a presentation? What do you do if you feel nervous? What are some things you try to do while you're giving your presentation?* Write some of the students' ideas on the board.

2. Go over the information about giving a presentation.

3. Check comprehension by asking questions: *What should you do before giving a presentation? What should you remember to do when you begin your presentation? What should you try to do during your presentation? Why?*

4. As you elicit answers to the questions in 3 above, write shortened versions on poster paper to post as presentation tips in the classroom.

▶ *Listening and Speaking 4, page 59*

A (15 minutes)
🔊 CD1, Track 34

1. Have a volunteer read the directions aloud.

2. Play the audio and have students note their suggestions as they listen.

3. Put students into pairs and have them come up with a list of suggestions for the speaker.

4. Have pairs trade lists and evaluate each other's advice. Have them focus on whether or not the advice would help the speaker with his presentation.

Activity A Answers, p. 59
Answers will vary. Possible answers: Don't say *Ummm…*. Don't start a sentence with *so* because it makes you sound unprepared. Don't ask yourself questions about where you were in the presentation. You use the word *really* a lot; try to use different, more academic-sounding vocabulary. Don't end your presentation with *that's it*.

B (25 minutes)

1. Read the directions to the class. Remind students about the advice they just wrote about giving a presentation. Provide note cards (if possible) so students can organize their ideas and make notes. As students work on their presentations, circulate and offer support.

2. Put students into pairs and have them give their presentations to each other. Ask partners to give feedback to each other using the information on page 58 as a guide.

 For additional practice with giving presentations, have students visit *Q Online Practice*.

Unit Assignment: Give a presentation to a group

Unit Question (5 minutes)

Refer students back to the ideas they discussed at the beginning of the unit about when children become adults. Cue students if necessary by asking specific questions about the content of the unit: *What events cause children to feel like adults? Is the transition always a positive transition? Why or why not? When is it positive?* Read the direction lines for the assignment together to ensure understanding.

Learning Outcome

1. Tie the Unit Assignment to the unit learning outcome. Say: *The outcome for this unit is to present a story describing an important event in your life that made you feel like an adult. This Unit Assignment is going to let you practice your speaking and organizational skills by giving a presentation to a small group.*

2. Explain that students will use a rubric similar to their Self-Assessment checklist on p. 62 to grade each other's Unit Assignments. You can also share a copy of the Unit Assignment Rubric (on p. 34 of this *Teacher's Handbook*) with the students.

Consider the Ideas

A (15 minutes)

🔊 CD1, Track 35

1. Read the directions aloud and preview the chart.
2. Have students take notes in the chart as you play the audio.

> **Consider the Ideas Answers, p. 60**
> Answers will vary. Possible answers:
> **1.** when she learned her mother had a problem with her brain
> **2.** the dream of traveling
> **3.** realized her mother needed her

B (10 minutes)

1. Students should work in pairs to review the notes they took and discuss any differences.
2. Elicit anwers from the class.

Prepare and Speak

Gather Ideas

A (10 minutes)

Direct students to use the graphic organizer to brainstorm about events in their lives that made them feel like more of an adult. Alternatively, students can write about the life of a friend or family member.

Tip for Success (1 minute)

1. Read the tip aloud.
2. Remind students that brainstorming means they do not edit or filter their ideas. They should write down everything that they think of related to the topic. They can get rid of the bad ideas later.

Organize Ideas

B (20 minutes)

1. Ask a volunteer to read the directions for Activity B. Preview the chart with students.
2. Have students complete numbers 1 and 2 individually. Then put students into pairs and have them practice their presentations until all of the questions in number 3 can be answered *yes*.
3. Circulate around the room to provide help and answer questions as needed.

Speak

C (30 minutes)

1. Go over the directions and the Self-Assessment checklist. Check for understanding: *What should you be thinking of while group members are giving their presentations?*
2. Use the Unit Assignment Rubric on page 34 to evaluate each student's presentation. Alternatively, give students copies of the Unit Assignment Rubric and have them assess each other as they give their presentations.

Alternative Unit Assignments

Assign or have students choose one of these assignments to do instead of, or in addition to, the Unit Assignment.

1. Read the following ideas about when someone becomes an adult. Then discuss the ideas in pairs and decide if you agree or disagree with them.

Idea 1. When you become financially independent or are fully employed, that is when you can call yourself adult.

Idea 2. I think you become an adult at 16.

2. There are many events which might mark the transition from child to adult, for example, getting a driving license, getting an apartment, or getting married. Work with classmates to brainstorm a list of qualities or characteristics that show a person is mature enough to do these activities and be considered an adult. Then work in pairs to do a role-play: one friend wants to do one of these activities, and the other friend gives advice on what to do to show others he or she is mature enough to do it.

 For an additional Unit Assignment, have students visit *Q Online Practice*.

Check and Reflect

Check

A (10 minutes)

1. Direct students to read and complete the Self-Assessment checklist.
2. Ask for a show of hands for how many students gave all or mostly *yes* answers.

3. Congratulate them on their success. Discuss the steps they can take if an item on the checklist was difficult for them. For example, if they had difficulty using correct sentence stress, encourage them to mark or underline important words in dialogs that they read in class.

Reflect

B (10 minutes)

Ask students to consider the questions in pairs or groups of three. When the conversations have died down, ask: *What new piece of information has stuck with you the most? How did your idea of when children become adults change as we progressed through the unit?*

▶ *Listening and Speaking 4, page 63*

Track Your Success (5 minutes)

1. Have students circle the words they have learned in this unit. Suggest that students go back through the unit to review any words they have forgotten.

2. Have students check the skills they have mastered. If students need more practice to feel confident about their proficiency in a skill, point out the page numbers and encourage them to review.

3. Read the learning outcome aloud *(Present a story describing an important event in your life that made you feel like an adult)*. Ask students if they feel that they have met the outcome.

Unit 3   Growing Up

Unit Assignment Rubric

Student name: _____

Date: _____

Unit Assignment: *Give a presentation to a group.*

20 points = Presentation element was completely successful (at least 90% of the time).
15 points = Presentation element was mostly successful (at least 70% of the time).
10 points = Presentation element was partially successful (at least 50% of the time).
 0 points = Presentation element was not successful.

Give a presentation to a group	20 points	15 points	10 points	0 points
Student spoke easily and clearly about an event in his or her life.				
Student made eye contact with the audience and used appropriate gestures.				
Student used sentence stress correctly.				
Student used vocabulary from the unit.				
Students used phrasal verbs correctly.				

Total points: _____

Comments:

UNIT 4

Unit QUESTION

How is health care changing?

Health Care

LISTENING • listening for reasons
VOCABULARY • collocations with verbs and nouns
GRAMMAR • past unreal conditionals
PRONUNCIATION • *can* and *can't*
SPEAKING • asking open-ended and follow-up questions

LEARNING OUTCOME

Participate in an interview about the advantages and disadvantages of medical tourism.

▶ *Listening and Speaking 4, page 65*

Preview the Unit

Learning Outcome

1. Ask a volunteer to read the unit skills and then the unit learning outcome.

2. Explain: *This is what you are expected to be able to do by the unit's end. The learning outcome explains how you are going to be evaluated. With this outcome in mind, you should focus on learning these skills (Listening, Vocabulary, Grammar, Pronunciation, Speaking) that will support your goal of participating in an interview about the advantages and disadvantages of medical tourism. This can also help you act as mentors in the classroom to help the other students meet this outcome.*

A (15 minutes)

1. Elicit students' ideas and feelings about health care and write them on the board.

2. Put students in pairs or small groups to discuss the first two questions.

3. Call on volunteers to share their ideas with the class. Ask: *Do you have a doctor you go to regularly? If so, how did you choose your doctor? How does cost affect your health care decisions? What is your opinion of health care in this country?*

4. Focus students' attention on the photo. Have a volunteer describe the photo to the class. Read the third question aloud. Elicit students' answers.

Activity A Answers, p. 65
Answers will vary. Possible answers:

1. I would find a new doctor by asking my friends and family for recommendations. Also, I would look on the Internet for recommendations.

2. I would go to a hospital that is very far away if it were cheaper. Cost is very important to me when selecting a hospital. / No, I would not go to a place that is very far away from my home. I want to be near my family when I am in the hospital.

B (15 minutes)

1. Introduce the Unit Question, *How is health care changing?* Ask related information questions or questions about personal experience to help students prepare for answering the more abstract Unit Question. Ask: *How do you think going to the doctor or to the hospital has changed in your lifetime? Do you spend more or less time with your doctors? Why or why not?*

2. Read the Unit Question aloud. Say: *Let's think about ways that health care is getting better or worse and why.*

3. Seat students in small groups and direct them to pass around a paper as quickly as they can, with each group member adding one item to the list. Tell them they have two minutes to make the lists and they should write as many ideas as possible.

4. Call time and ask a reporter from each group to read the list aloud.

5. Use items from the list as a springboard for discussion. For example: *From our lists, we see people think going to the doctor has become easier and faster. Is there anything doctors and hospitals could do to make the experience even easier?*

Activity B Answers, p. 65

Answers will vary. Possible answers: Health care is becoming more expensive. / There is new technology in health care, so doctors are able to cure more diseases. / Health care is getting worse because doctors have less time to listen to their patients.

The Q Classroom

CD2, Track 2

1. Play The Q Classroom. Use the example from the audio to help students continue the conversation. Ask: *How did the students answer the question? What do you think about their ideas?*

2. Yuna notes that there are more specialists than there used to be in the health care field. Ask: *What's a specialist? Do you agree with Yuna? If so, do you think that is a good thing? Are specialists better for a patient than general doctors? Why or why not?*

▶ *Listening and Speaking 4, page 66*

C (10 minutes)

1. Ask a volunteer to read the directions aloud. Remind students that they should choose their preferred characteristics individually and then discuss their choices with a partner.

2. After pairs have discussed their answers, have the class focus on the characteristics they found to be most important. Ask: *Why are these characteristics so important?* Also, elicit which characteristics were the least important. Ask: *Why aren't these characteristics as important?*

D (15 minutes)

1. Read the directions aloud. Have students work in pairs to discuss the questions. Then group pairs together and have them share their answers with each other.

2. As larger groups work together, walk around the room and listen to their answers. Select a few model answers and ask those students to share their thoughts with the class.

Activity D Answers, p. 66

Answers will vary. Possible answers:
1. I wouldn't travel to another country because I can't afford it. / I would travel to another country because it would be cheaper, and I'd get a vacation.
2. I would go to Mexico because it is close, and I am from that country. / I would go to Thailand because I hear that the doctors there are very good.

LISTENING

▶ *Listening and Speaking 4, page 67*

LISTENING 1:
Vacation, Adventure, and Surgery?

VOCABULARY (15 minutes)

1. Ask volunteers to read each vocabulary word and its definition.

2. Answer any questions about meaning and provide examples of the words in context. Pronounce each word and have students repeat.

3. Have students work in pairs to complete the sentences with the correct words.

4. Call on volunteers to read the sentences aloud.

MULTILEVEL OPTION

Have higher-level students write an additional sample sentence for each word or expression. Have volunteers write their sentences on the board. Correct the sentences with the whole class, focusing on the use of the word or expression rather than other grammatical issues.

Vocabulary Answers, pp. 67–68
1. procedure; **2.** standard; **3.** image;
4. state-of-the-art; **5.** access; **6.** exports;
7. practice; **8.** luxurious; **9.** deteriorate;
10. environment

 For additional practice with the vocabulary, have students visit *Q Online Practice.*

Listening and Speaking 4, page 68

PREVIEW LISTENING 1 (5 minutes)

1. Read the introduction aloud and direct students to complete the activity.

2. Tell students they should review their answer(s) after listening.

Preview Listening 1 Answer, p. 68
Answers will vary.

Listening 1 Background Note

Individuals aren't the only ones concerned about cost when it comes to meeting health care needs—so are governments. The Peace Corps is a United States government organization that sends volunteers to various countries to help in fields such as education, agriculture, and business. When volunteers need medical treatment, the Peace Corps may send them to countries such as Thailand because the cost for such treatment is less expensive than in the U.S. or other countries and the level of care is just as good.

Teaching Note

Students may find the following words/phrases difficult:

RV: (noun) *abbreviation for "recreational vehicle"; a large vehicle that you can sleep, cook, etc. in when you are traveling or on vacation*

bypass: (noun) *a medical operation to create a new passage for blood to flow through, especially near the heart*

cardiologist: (noun) *a doctor who specializes in the study and treatment of heart disorders*

RN: (noun) *the abbreviation for "registered nurse"; a person who has official permission to work as a nurse*

malpractice: (noun) *wrong or bad treatment or service, especially by a doctor or a lawyer*

chemotherapy: (noun) *the treatment of disease, especially cancer, with the use of chemical substances*

plastic surgery: (noun) *surgical operations to repair or replace damaged skin or to improve the appearance of a person's face or body*

convalesce: (verb) *to spend time recovering after an illness*

LISTEN FOR MAIN IDEAS (10 minutes)

CD2, Track 3

1. Ask students to preview the statements and answer choices.

2. Play the audio. Ask students to complete the activity on their own.

3. Elicit the answers from volunteers.

> **Listen for Main Ideas Answers, pp. 68–69**
> **1.** b;   **2.** a;   **3.** a;   **4.** c

Listening and Speaking 4, page 69

LISTEN FOR DETAILS (15 minutes)

CD2, Track 4

1. Direct students to preview the statements. Play the audio and have them complete the activity.

2. Have students compare answers with a partner.

3. Play the audio again so students can check their answers.

4. Go over the answers with the class. Elicit corrections for the false statements.

> **Listen for Details Answers, p. 69**
> **1.** F;   **2.** F;   **3.** F;   **4.** T;   **5.** F;   **6.** F;   **7.** T;   **8.** T

 For additional practice with listening comprehension, have students visit *Q Online Practice*.

WHAT DO YOU THINK? (10 minutes)

1. Ask students to read the questions and reflect on their answers.

2. Seat students in small groups and assign roles: a group leader to make sure everyone contributes, a note-taker to record the group's ideas, a reporter to share the group's ideas with the class, and a timekeeper to watch the clock.

3. Give students five minutes to discuss the questions. Call time if conversations are winding down. Allow extra time if necessary.

4. Call on each group's reporter to share ideas with the class.

> **What Do You Think? Answers, p. 69**
> Answers will vary. Possible answers:
> **1.** One negative aspect of medical tourism is that because so many foreigners go to those countries for care, the medical care costs for citizens of the countries are too high. Another negative aspect is that if the surgeries do not go well, the patients may have more problems than they would in the U.S.
> **2.** I think that hospitals should try to attract patients from other countries because those patients are willing to pay a lot of money for certain surgeries. / I think that hospitals shouldn't advertise to patients from other countries. Hospitals should help the local people who need medical care.

▶ *Listening and Speaking 4, page 70*

Listening Skill:
Listening for reasons (10 minutes)

CD2, Track 5

1. Go over the information in the skill box. Play the audio as noted.

2. Check comprehension by asking questions: *How do speakers signal they are about to give reasons for one of their ideas? Why do speakers need to give reasons? Do reasons come before or after a statement about an action, condition, or event?*

A (10 minutes)

CD2, Track 6

1. Ask a volunteer to read the directions. Preview the chart with students.

2. Play the audio and have students complete the task.

3. Have students compare answers with a partner. Then check the answers as a class.

> **Activity A Answers, p. 70**
> **1.** Because it was too expensive
> **2.** Because he could afford surgery in Thailand
> **3.** Because labor and malpractice insurance is cheap
> **4.** Because people don't like to go to hospitals
> **5.** She wanted to pay less for her surgery. She didn't have insurance in the U.S. Also, she wanted to have a surgery that isn't approved in the U.S.

▶ *Listening and Speaking 4, page 71*

B (10 minutes)

Have a volunteer read the directions. Pair students and have them give reasons for each situation. Discuss the reasons as a class.

> **Activity B Answers, p. 71**
> Answers will vary.

Skill Note

Actively listening for reasons is an important tool to becoming an efficient listener. By knowing where the reasons might appear in a speech or conversation—and knowing some verbal clues that might hint that a reason is coming—a listener can be judicious when deciding which information to pay attention to.

 For additional practice with listening for reasons, have students visit *Q Online Practice*.

Critical Thinking Tip (1 minute)

1. Have a volunteer read the tip aloud.

2. Explain: *Using what you have learned will help you remember new words and information better. If you can use what you have learned, you increase your chances of retaining that information.*

Critical Q: Expansion Activity

Use What You've Learned

Ask students to brainstorm situations in which they can use the language or skills they're learning in this unit or have learned in previous units. Encourage them to flip through the book to look at previous lessons. Have students share their ideas with the class.

Develop a plan with students where for a week, they purposefully try to use the language they are learning outside of the classroom.

Check in with students in a week to discuss their successes and challenges with this task.

Learning Outcome

Use the learning outcome to frame the purpose and relevance of Listening 1. Ask: *What did you learn from Listening 1 that prepares you to participate in an interview about the advantages and disadvantages of medical tourism?* (Students learned why some people went to other countries for medical care and what their experiences were like. This information may help them in their interviews.)

LISTENING 2:
Medical Travel Can Create Problems

VOCABULARY (15 minutes)

1. Direct students to read the vocabulary words and definitions. Ask: *What words do you already know? What do those words mean?*

2. Answer any questions about meaning and provide examples of the words in context. Model the pronunciation of the words and have students repeat.

3. Pair students and have them complete the sentences.

4. Ask volunteers to read the sentences aloud.

> **Vocabulary Answers, pp. 71–72**
> **1.** obligation;   **2.** skilled;   **3.** focus;
> **4.** facility;   **5.** private sector;   **6.** resign;
> **7.** shortage;   **8.** typical;   **9.** found;
> **10.** rural;   **11.** benefit;   **12.** resident

MULTILEVEL OPTION

Have higher-level students write three sentences with two or three vocabulary words in each one, while lower-level students write three sentences with only one vocabulary word in each one.

 For additional practice with the vocabulary, have students visit *Q Online Practice*.

▶ *Listening and Speaking 4, page 73*

PREVIEW LISTENING 2 (10 minutes)

1. Read the introduction to the class.

2. Have students complete the activity in pairs. After the discussion has died down, ask a few volunteers to share their answers with the class.

3. Have students review their answers after listening.

> **Preview Listening 2 Answer, p. 73**
> Answers will vary. Possible answers: Medical tourism can cause residents of these countries to not be able to find affordable care. Medical tourism can cause specialists to only work with tourists and not help residents of these countries.

Listening 2 Background Note

One of the negative consequences of medical tourism might prove to be deadly. Recently, "superbugs"— "bugs" that are becoming resistant to antibiotics— have sickened people travelling from one country to another. The fear is that people seeking medical treatment in other countries might be increasingly susceptible to catching these "superbugs" and carrying them back to their home countries. Experts worry that an increase in medical tourism might increase the circulation of these bugs in international populations.

LISTEN FOR MAIN IDEAS (10 minutes)

 CD2, Track 7

1. Choose a student to read the directions aloud. Give students a minute or two to read the sentences.

2. Play the audio as students listen and complete the activity.

3. Check answers as a class. Elicit corrections for the false statements.

> **Listen for Main Ideas Answers, p. 73**
> **1.** T; **2.** F; **3.** T; **4.** F; **5.** F; **6.** T; **7.** T; **8.** T

Listening and Speaking 4, page 74

LISTEN FOR DETAILS (10 minutes)

CD2, Track 8

1. Direct students to preview the questions. Play the audio again as students complete the activity.

2. Have students compare answers with a partner.

3. Go over the answers with the class.

Listen for Details Answers, p. 74
1. 75%
2. He wanted to found a hospital that would serve the basic needs of the people of Thailand and train doctors. He did this after his son died.
3. Private hospitals are modern, and doctors can make more money in private hospitals.
4. Specialists like surgeons
5. The main difference is that Bumrungrad has modern medical equipment.
6. They think these countries will find a balance between serving medical tourists and serving the local population.

 For additional practice with listening comprehension, have students visit *Q Online Practice*.

WHAT DO YOU THINK?

A (15 minutes)

1. Ask students to read the questions and reflect on their answers.

2. Seat students in small groups and assign roles: a group leader to make sure everyone contributes, a note-taker to record the group's ideas, a reporter to share the group's ideas with the class, and a timekeeper to watch the clock.

3. Give students five minutes to discuss the questions. Call time if conversations are winding down.

4. Call on each group's reporter to share their groups' answers with the class.

> **Activity A Answers, p. 74**
> Answers will vary. Possible answers:
> **1.** All residents should have access to Bumrungrad hospital at a reduced price because these private hospitals should also serve the local population. The hospital should try to serve the local population by offering cheaper services for them.
> **2.** Earning more money at a private hospital would help me support my family. However, I also want to help the local people, so I would work at the public hospital, too.

B (10 minutes)

1. Tell the students that they should think about both Listening 1 and Listening 2 as they answer the questions in Activity B.

2. Ask students to discuss their answers in their groups.

3. Call on volunteers to share ideas with the class.

Activity B Answers, p. 74
Answers will vary. Possible answers:
1. I think it is good that people have the option to go to another country for a medical procedure because it is much cheaper. If you don't have insurance, the cost of medical care in the United States is enormous. / I think the only way these hospitals can get patients is to try to attract people to go there.
2. I believe that schools are obligated to serve the poor. Everyone should have the same opportunity to get an education.

Learning Outcome

Use the learning outcome to frame the purpose and relevance of Listenings 1 and 2. Ask: *What did you learn from Listenings 1 and 2 that prepares you to participate in an interview about the advantages and disadvantages of medical tourism?* (Students learned about the advantages and disadvantages of medical tourism. These ideas may help them in their interviews.)

▶ *Listening and Speaking 4, page 75*

Vocabulary Skill: Collocations with verbs and nouns (15 minutes)

1. Read the title of the skill. Probe for previous knowledge. Ask: *Have you heard of collocations before? Do you know any?*

2. Ask a volunteer read the explanation of this vocabulary skill to the class. Go over the examples together.

3. Check comprehension: *Which word usually collocates with* surgery? *What will learning collocations help you do?*

Skill Note

When students learn a new vocabulary word, encourage them to note other words that it collocates with. This will help them integrate the new word into their productive language.

EXPANSION ACTIVITY: Creating Dialogues
(15 minutes)

1. Call up the online corpus you used in Unit 2 of this *Teacher's Handbook*. Alternately, have available several dictionaries that provide collocations.

2. Provide a list of nouns from this unit's vocabulary sections. Ask students to look them up in the online corpus or in a dictionary and note which

words they are commonly used with.

3. Have students create and act out a short dialogue using a few of the collocations they found.

A (10 minutes)

1. Have students work individually to complete the activity. Pair students to compare answers.

2. Go over the answers with the class. Elicit example sentences using some of the collocations.

Activity A Answers, p. 75
1. had; 2. make; 3. had; 4. make; 5. take; 6. take

▶ *Listening and Speaking 4, page 76*

B (10 minutes)
))) CD2, Track 9

1. Direct students to preview the sentences and consider what verb might be missing from each.

2. Play the audio track and have students fill in the missing words that they hear.

3. Have students share answers in pairs. Then go over the answers with the class.

Activity B Answers, p. 76
1. creating;   2. takes;   3. do;   4. see;
5. had;   6. found;   7. make;   8. have

Tip for Success (2 minutes)

1. Have a volunteer read the tip aloud.

2. Ask the students to open their dictionaries and see if they contain collocations for words. If they do, ask students to look at these collocations when they are looking up the definitions for new words.

C (15 minutes)

1. Direct students to write their sentences individually. Then have students share their sentences with a partner.

2. Circulate around the room and offer support as needed. Select a few students whose sentences will serve as good examples for the class.

3. Ask volunteers to write their sentences on the board.

Activity C Answers, p. 76
Answers will vary.

 For additional practice with collocations with verbs and nouns, have students visit *Q Online Practice*.

▶ *Listening and Speaking 4, page 77*

SPEAKING

Grammar:
Past unreal conditionals (15 minutes)

1. Present the information in the grammar skill box. Ask volunteers to read some of the examples. Point out the difference in certainty between *would* vs. *could/might*.

2. Write *If I had been born 100 years earlier, I would have...* on the board and give some sample responses (e.g., *...worn handmade clothes, ...been a better cook).*

3. Ask students to complete the sentence, drawing their attention to the past perfect in the *if* clause and the use of *would/could/might have* plus past participle.

Skill Note

Past unreal conditionals can be difficult for English learners, but it is an important skill to learn. By asking students to reflect on things they would have liked to have done in the past, the concept of past unreal conditions can be easier to understand.

A (10 minutes)

1. Direct students to read the directions and complete the activity individually.

2. Call on volunteers to share their answers.

> **Activity A Answers, pp. 77–78**
> **1.** N; **2.** N; **3.** N; **4.** Y; **5.** Y; **6.** N; **7.** N; **8.** N

▶ *Listening and Speaking 4, page 78*

B (20 minutes)

1. Direct students to complete the activity individually.

2. In pairs, students should read each conditional sentence, checking each others' answers.

3. Ask volunteers to write the sentences on the board. Correct them as a class. Point out that in number 2, the main clause uses *would not hurt* because Paolo's knee still hurts.

> **Activity B Answers, p. 78**
> **1.** If Melanie had studied, she would have passed the exam.
> **2.** If Paulo had had surgery, his knee would not still hurt.

3. If we had known James was sick, we would/could have taken him to the doctor.
4. If I had brought a map, I would/could have found the hotel.
5. If you hadn't missed your last appointment, you would/could have gotten a blood test.
6. If Cristina hadn't fallen down, she wouldn't have hurt her leg.
7. If Stephanie Sedlmayr had had surgery in the U.S., it would have cost her over $10,000.

 For additional practice with past unreal conditionals, have students visit *Q Online Practice.*

▶ *Listening and Speaking 4, page 79*

Pronunciation:
Can and *can't* (15 minutes)

🔊 CD2, Track 10

1. Write the words *can* and *can't* on the board. Ask students: *How do you pronounce these two words?* Now, write these sentences: *I can hear you. / I can't hear you.* Ask students: *How do you say these sentences?* Pay attention to how students pronounce *can* and *can't.*

2. Present the information in the pronunciation skill box and play the audio when noted. Ask: *How does the pronunciation of these two words change when they are in sentences? What does* can *sound like when it begins a sentence?*

3. Ask students to read the two sentences on the board again. Then say a few of the sentences from Activity A. Have students raise their left hand if they hear *can* and their right hand if they hear *can't.*

A (10 minutes)
🔊 CD2, Track 11

1. Have students read the directions.

2. Play the audio track and ask students to circle the word they hear.

3. Go over the answers with the class.

> **Activity A Answers, p. 79**
> **1.** can; **2.** can; **3.** can; **4.** can't; **5.** can;
> **6.** can't; **7.** can't; **8.** can; **9.** can; **10.** can't

▶ *Listening and Speaking 4, page 80*

B (10 minutes)

1. Have students read the directions and match the statements with the correct responses.

2. To check answers, choose students to perform the conversations in front of the classroom. Reinforce the pronunciation of *can* and *can't* as needed.

Activity B Answers, p. 80
1. You can come with me. Thanks. / You can't come with me. Why not?
2. She can speak French. So can I. / She can't speak French. Neither can I.
3. Dr. Lee can see you now. I'll be right in. / Dr. Lee can't see you now. I'll come back later.
4. I can be there at 3:00. Great. I'll see you then. / I can't be there at 3:00. Then we'll have to reschedule.
5. Grace said she can swim. Great! Let's go swimming. / Grace said she can't swim. I'll teach her.
6. James can afford a vacation. Good. He needs the time off. / James can't afford a vacation. That's too bad. He needs the time off.

 For additional practice with *can* and *can't*, have students visit *Q Online Practice*.

Speaking Skill:
Asking open-ended questions (15 minutes)

1. Choose four higher-level volunteers who'd like to teach their classmates about open-ended questions. Sit them together and have them read the information about open-ended questions on page 80. (Alternatively, have them do this for homework.)

2. While those four volunteers are working, briefly review *yes/no* questions with the class and point out how they can stop conversations from continuing.

3. Divide the classroom into four groups, assigning one of the four volunteers to each group. Give these four volunteers five minutes to teach their groups about open-ended questions.

4. As a class, go over the information in the skill box. Elicit open-ended questions from volunteers to show that they understood the information.

5. Check comprehension by asking questions: *Are yes/no questions open-ended? Why are open-ended questions important in conversations?*

Skill Note

Yes/no questions are good for extracting information, but they do not encourage conversation. Asking open-ended questions is a great way for students to practice listening and speaking with others. Show students how they can use open-ended follow-up questions to expand on *yes/no* questions. For example:

Do you have siblings? What was it like growing up with them?

Do you like going to the doctor? Why not?

▶ *Listening and Speaking 4, page 81*

A (15 minutes)

1. Have students work individually to complete the activity. Pair students to practice asking and answering the new questions.

2. Call on volunteers to read their questions.

Activity A Answers, p. 81
Answers will vary. Possible answers:
1. How did you feel before you had surgery?
2. What was it like to stay in the hospitals?
3. What kinds of problems is medical tourism causing in India?
4. Why is health care cheaper in other places?
5. Why is your doctor a good physician?
6. What are hospitals like in this city?

B (10 minutes)
🔊 CD2, Track 12
1. Read the directions aloud.
2. Pause the audio after you play each excerpt to give students time to write a follow-up question. Allow students to work in pairs.
3. Have students share their follow-up questions with the class.

Activity B Answers, p. 81
Answers will vary. Possible answers:
1. Why don't people want to go to a hospital?
2. How can they see 350,000 patients a year?
3. Why is India a good destination for medical tourism?

MULTILEVEL OPTION

Have lower-level students read their revised interviews aloud, and have higher-level students predict what the interviewees' answer to the new, follow-up question might be.

21ST CENTURY SKILLS

In the workplace, employees are often called upon to make judgments and decisions in real time. Employers value people who can quickly analyze and evaluate information and alternate points of view in order to propose a solution for one's team or company. To be able to look at a question, problem, or situation and weigh the pros and cons against desired outcomes is a skill that will help students make sound decisions quickly. The skills covered in this chapter feed into the macro skill of quickly making and communicating decisions in the workplace or the classroom.

▶ *Listening and Speaking 4, page 82*

Unit Assignment: Conduct an interview

Unit Question (5 minutes)

Refer students back to the ideas they discussed at the beginning of the unit about how health care is changing. Cue students if necessary by asking specific questions about the content of the unit: *Do you think health care in this country is changing? Why or why not? How is health care changing? What is different about health care now than 10 or 20 years ago?* Read the directions for the assignment together to ensure understanding.

Learning Outcome

1. Tie the Unit Assignment to the unit learning outcome. Say: *The outcome for this unit is to participate in an interview about the advantages and disadvantages of medical tourism. This Unit Assignment is going to let you practice your speaking and organizational skills by conducting an interview. You will also practice using collocations, pronouncing* can *and* can't, *and asking open-ended and follow-up questions.*

2. Explain that you are going to use a rubric similar to their Self-Assessment checklist on p. 84 to grade their Unit Assignments. You can also share a copy of the Unit Assignment Rubric (on p. 45 of this *Teacher's Handbook*) with the students.

Consider the Ideas

A (20 minutes)

1. Write the words *for* and *against* on the board and explain that *for* is the positive side of an argument and *against* is the negative side. Write the topic *medical tourism* and have students think of its positive and negative aspects.

2. Have students read the directions for this activity. Put students into groups and have them decide whether or not they would recommend medical tourism to their close friend, listing the reasons that they mention in their notebooks.

3. Briefly discuss as a class the students' *for* and *against* arguments.

Prepare and Speak

Gather Ideas

A (10 minutes)

1. Ask students to read the statements and determine if they are for or against medical tourism.

2. Discuss students' ideas as a class.

Listening and Speaking 4, page 83

Organize Ideas

B (15 minutes)

1. Ask a volunteer to read the directions for Activity B. Preview the chart with students.

2. Have students complete the chart individually. Then put students into pairs and have them share their ideas with each other.

3. Elicit ideas from the class. You may want to recreate the chart on the board.

▶ *Listening and Speaking 4, page 84*

Speak

C (45 minutes)

1. Go over the directions and ask students to preview the Self-Assessment checklist on p. 84 before they begin this activity. Check for understanding by asking: *There are three roles in this interview. What are they? Who are you writing questions for? Who are you writing answers for? How long should each answer be?*

2. Ask students to practice their interviews in their groups before they present to the class.

3. Then have each group present their interview to the class. Use the Unit Assignment Rubric on page 45 to evaluate each student.

4. Alternatively, have each group present to one or two other groups rather than the whole class, and direct the students that are listening to give scores based upon the rubric on page 45 of this *Teacher's Handbook*. Make sure that students have adequate copies of the rubric to use.

Alternative Unit Assignments

Assign or have students choose one of these assignments to do instead of, or in addition to, the Unit Assignment.

1. Devise a plan to do online research to find a doctor or medical facility in another country. Consider the pros and cons of receiving medical treatment in that country. Share your plan and concerns in a small group.

2. There are a variety of treatment options and medicines available for some diseases and medical problems. Some of these are available through a doctor's office or medical facility, while some are only available online or at special stores. What types of medicine or medical advice would you be comfortable getting online? What are the advantages and disadvantages of taking care of a medical problem this way?

 For an additional Unit Assignment, have students visit *Q Online Practice*.

Check and Reflect

Check

A (10 minutes)

1. Direct students to read and complete the Self-Assessment checklist.

2. Ask for a show of hands for how many students gave all or mostly *yes* answers.

3. Congratulate them on their success. Discuss the steps they can take if an item on the checklist was difficult for them. For example, if they didn't ask open-ended or follow-up questions, encourage them to practice asking these types of questions any time they have a discussion with others in class.

Reflect

B (10 minutes)

Ask students to consider the questions in pairs or groups. When the conversations have died down, ask: *What new piece of information has stuck with you the most? How did your idea of how health care is changing expand as we progressed through the unit?*

▶ *Listening and Speaking 4, page 85*

Track Your Success (5 minutes)

1. Have students circle the words they have learned in this unit. Suggest that students go back through the unit to review any words they have forgotten.

2. Have students check the skills they have mastered. If students need more practice to feel confident about their proficiency in a skill, point out the page numbers and encourage them to review.

3. Read the learning outcome aloud (*Participate in an interview about the advantages and disadvantages of medical tourism*). Ask students if they feel that they have met the outcome.

Unit Assignment Rubric

Student name: _____

Date: _____

Unit Assignment: *Conduct an interview.*

20 points = Interview element was completely successful (at least 90% of the time).
15 points = Interview element was mostly successful (at least 70% of the time).
10 points = Interview element was partially successful (at least 50% of the time).
  0 points = Interview element was not successful.

Conduct an Interview	20 points	15 points	10 points	0 points
Student spoke easily and clearly in the interview.				
Student gave logical reasons for his or her opinion on medical tourism (or, for the interviewer, asked logical questions).				
Student asked open-ended and follow-up questions.				
Student used collocations with nouns and verbs correctly.				
Student pronounced *can* and *can't* correctly.				

Total points: _____

Comments:

Unit QUESTION
What makes a work of art popular?

Art Today

LISTENING • making inferences
VOCABULARY • word forms
GRAMMAR • present perfect and present perfect continuous
PRONUNCIATION • basic intonation patterns
SPEAKING • avoiding answering questions

LEARNING OUTCOME

Role-play a conversation expressing personal opinions about what makes art popular.

▶ *Listening and Speaking 4, page 87*
Preview the Unit

Learning Outcome

1. Ask a volunteer to read the unit skills and then the unit learning outcome.

2. Explain: *This is what you are expected to be able to do by the unit's end. The learning outcome explains how you are going to be evaluated. With this outcome in mind, you should focus on learning these skills (Listening, Vocabulary, Grammar, Pronunciation, Speaking) that will support your goal of role-playing a conversation expressing personal opinions about what makes art popular. This can also help you act as mentors in the classroom to help the other students meet this outcome.*

A (15 minutes)

1. Choose a few pictures of popular pieces of art. Display them around the room and ask students to walk around and look at them. Alternatively, play music or show pictures from different films. Give students small slips of paper to write down their impressions of the artwork (or music / films). Ask: *Do you like the pieces? Why? Why not?*

2. Put students in pairs or small groups to discuss the first two questions.

3. Call on volunteers to share their ideas with the class. Ask: *What is art? What makes a painting or a movie or a book art? Have you ever made art?*

4. Focus students' attention on the photo. Have a volunteer describe the photo to the class. Read the third question aloud. Elicit students' answers.

Activity A Answers, p. 87
Answers will vary. Possible answers:
1. When I hear the word *art,* I think of expensive paintings and museums. / Art makes me think of my mom, who paints in her studio every day.
2. My favorite book is *One Hundred Years of Solitude* by Gabriel Garcia Marquez. The best thing about it is how it describes people.
3. The artist is drawing a famous painting on the sidewalk.

B (15 minutes)

1. Introduce the Unit Question, *What makes a work of art popular?* Ask related information questions or questions about personal experience to help students prepare for answering the more abstract Unit Question: *What art do you like? Why do you like it? Do other people like it? Why or why not?*

2. Tell the students: *Let's start off our discussion by listing reasons why a work of art might become popular. For example, we could start our list with "shows something famous" because many people like art that shows a famous scene—like the pyramids of Egypt or the Eiffel Tower. What else can make art popular?*

3. Seat students in small groups and direct them to pass around a paper as quickly as they can, with each group member adding one item to the list. Tell them they have two minutes to make the lists and they should write as many ideas as possible.

4. Call time and ask a reporter from each group to read the list aloud.

5. Use items from the list as a springboard for discussion. For example: *From our lists, we see that art can become popular because people like things that media sources (e.g., newspapers, magazines, TV) say are popular. How does the media help decide what is popular?*

Activity B Answers, p. 87

Answers will vary. Possible answers: Art becomes popular when many people like it. / Art becomes popular if it means something special to many people. / It's hard to say what makes art popular.

The Q Classroom

CD2, Track 13

1. Play The Q Classroom. Use the example from the audio to help students continue the conversation. Ask: *How did the students answer the question? Do you agree or disagree with their ideas? Why?*

2. In the audio, Sophy notes that people just like art that "looks nice." Ask: *Do you agree? Does popular art have to look "nice"? What does* nice *mean?*

▶ *Listening and Speaking 4, page 88*

C (10 minutes)

1. Ask a volunteer to read the directions. Preview the survey to ensure understanding.

2. Direct students to complete the survey. Place students into pairs and ask them to share their answers. Ask: *Which choices did neither of you consider to be art? Why not? Which choices did you both consider to be art? Why?*

D (10 minutes)

1. Ask a volunteer to read the directions aloud. Have students make notes about their answers in their notebooks.

2. Group students together and have them discuss their responses.

3. Elicit answers from the class.

MULTILEVEL OPTION

Pair lower- and higher-level students. Have the higher-level students interview the lower-level students to complete Activity D. The higher-level student will record the lower-level partner's answer and share it with the class.

▶ *Listening and Speaking 4, page 89*

LISTENING

LISTENING 1:
Manga's New Popularity

VOCABULARY (20 minutes)

1. Read the directions aloud. Ask students to read each vocabulary word and its definition. Answer any questions about meaning and provide examples of the words in context. Model the pronunciation of each vocabulary word.

2. Put students in pairs to complete the sentences.

3. Ask volunteers to read the sentences.

4. Ask questions to help students connect with the vocabulary: *How do you **recall** information in school? What newspapers are in **circulation** in your area? What television or book **series** do you like?*

Vocabulary Answers, pp. 89–90
1. panel;   **2.** recall;   **3.** convention;
4. take note of;   **5.** appreciation;   **6.** series;
7. breed;   **8.** encounter;   **9.** development;
10. circulation;   **11.** expand;   **12.** generation

MULTILEVEL OPTION

Ask higher-level students to write five sentences using at least five of the vocabulary words. Then have them share their sentences with a partner. Pair lower-level students to write three sentences with at least three of the vocabulary words.

 For additional practice with the vocabulary, have students visit *Q Online Practice*.

▶ *Listening and Speaking 4, page 90*

PREVIEW LISTENING 1 (5 minutes)

1. Read the introduction and ask students to complete the activity.

2. Tell students they should review their answer(s) after listening.

Preview Listening 1 Answer, p. 90
Answers will vary.

Listening 1 Background Note

Comic book conventions or fairs are popular all over the world. One of the most well-known is Comiket, which is held twice annually in Tokyo, Japan. Begun in 1975, comic book writers from all over the world come to Comiket to sell their works because it is the largest convention that focuses on self-published comic books. What this means is that anyone who writes and produces their own comic can sell their work at this convention. Another popular comic book convention is Comic-Con International: San Diego, held in the United States. Comic-Con has been held anually in California since the 1970s.

▶ *Listening and Speaking 4, page 91*

LISTEN FOR MAIN IDEAS (10 minutes)

 CD2, Track 14

1. Ask students to read the directions and preview the questions and answers.

2. Play the audio and have students circle the correct answers.

3. Ask volunteers to share their answers. If necessary, play the audio again so that students can check their answers.

> **Listen For Main Ideas Answers, p. 91**
> **1.** b; **2.** a; **3.** b; **4.** b

LISTEN FOR DETAILS (10 minutes)

 CD2, Track 15

1. Direct students to read the directions and statements.

2. Play the audio again and direct them to label the statements *T* for true or *F* for false.

3. Have students compare answers with a partner.

4. Go over the answers with the class. Elicit corrections for the false statements.

> **Listen for Details Answers, p. 91**
> **1.** F; **2.** T; **3.** F; **4.** F; **5.** T; **6.** T

For additional practice with listening comprehension, have students visit *Q Online Practice*.

▶ *Listening and Speaking 4, page 92*

 WHAT DO YOU THINK? (15 minutes)

1. Ask students to read the questions and reflect on their answers.

2. Seat students in small groups and assign roles: a group leader to make sure everyone contributes, a note-taker to record the group's ideas, a reporter to share the group's ideas with the class, and a timekeeper to watch the clock.

3. Give students ten minutes to discuss the questions. Call time if conversations are winding down. Allow them an extra minute or two if necessary.

4. Call on each group's reporter to share ideas with the class.

> **What Do You Think? Answers, p. 92**
> Answers will vary. Possible answers:
> **1.** People enjoy reading manga because they can connect with the characters in the stories. Also, they enjoy the artwork.
> **2.** I think that schools should use manga in the classroom because it is a fun way to get students involved in reading. / I don't think students should read manga in school because the stories are not always appropriate for them.
> **3.** One possible negative effect is that libraries might not have enough resources to keep other more traditional books in circulation.

Learning Outcome

Use the learning outcome to frame the purpose and relevance of Listening 1. Ask: *What did you learn from Listening 1 that prepares you to role-play a conversation expressing personal opinions about what makes art popular?* (Students learned why manga is popular. They may want to use these ideas in their role-plays.)

Listening Skill: Making inferences
(15 minutes)

 CD2, Track 16

1. Read the first paragraph in the skill box. Play the audio of the excerpt. Read the inference and discuss any words or phrases in the excerpt that support the inference.

2. Read the information about a speaker's attitude or emotions.

3. Check comprehension by asking questions: *What do you do when you make inferences? What clues should you pay attention to when trying to infer a speaker's feelings?*

Inferring a speaker's meaning can be difficult, but those who excel at doing so have an advantage over those who cannot. In the workplace, employees may need to make inferences from meetings or discussions with colleagues or superiors. For example, they may need to infer a plan of action based on something that was discussed. Talk with students about the benefits of making inferences at work and when it might be important to check their inferences with someone before taking action.

EXPANSION ACTIVITY: Inferring from Pictures (15 minutes)

1. Place students into groups of four and provide them with pictures (like those suggested below) to practice making inferences.

   a. Provide students with a series of pictures of people and have them make inferences about their lives.

   b. Show a few pictures of people's faces and ask students to infer how the people feel.

2. Have students share with the class what they inferred from these pictures. Ensure that they support their opinions with evidence from the pictures or their own experiences.

▶ *Listening and Speaking 4, page 93*

A (10 minutes)

CD2, Track 17

1. Preview the inferences with students. Ask volunteers to read the questions and statements aloud.

2. Play the audio and direct students to select their choices. Discuss the answers as a class.

   Activity A Answers, p. 93
   1. a;　**2.** a;　**3.** b

B (10 minutes)

CD2, Track 18

1. Preview the task. Play the audio again and ask students to select their answers, noting that some items may have more than one correct answer.

2. Elicit the answers from volunteers.

   Activity B Answers, p. 93
   1. b;　**2.** b, c;　**3.** a;　**4.** a, c

Tip for Success (2 minutes)

1. Ask a volunteer to read the tip aloud.

2. Ask: *How do you think making inferences can help when preparing for tests? Have you ever made inferences when taking a test? How did it help you?*

 For additional practice with making inferences, have students visit *Q Online Practice*.

▶ *Listening and Speaking 4, page 94*

LISTENING 2: Thomas Kinkade

VOCABULARY (20 minutes)

1. Read the directions aloud. Direct students to read each sentence and try to guess the meaning of the word in bold first. Remind them to use context clues. Then they should write the word next to the correct definition.

2. Call on volunteers to share their answers.

3. Model the pronunciation of each vocabulary word and have students repeat. Listen for correct syllable stress.

   Vocabulary Answers, pp. 94–95
   a. identify with;　**b.** clone;　**c.** regard;
   d. reproduction;　**e.** marketing;　**f.** gallery;
   g. amateur;　**h.** unique;　**i.** operation;
   j. overseas

MULTILEVEL OPTION

Group lower-level students and assist them with the task. Provide alternate example sentences to help them understand the words. For example, *He is an **amateur** painter. He just paints for fun in his free time. Children can **identify with** the characters in books because the characters do the same things that children do. The **gallery** is showing some new paintings tomorrow night.*

 For additional practice with the vocabulary, have students visit *Q Online Practice*.

▶ *Listening and Speaking 4, page 95*

PREVIEW LISTENING 2 (5 minutes)

1. Read the introduction. Direct students to look at the painting. Ask: *What do you see in the picture? Why do you think his paintings are popular?*

2. Ask students to consider the question and check their reasons. Ask volunteers to brainstorm other reasons why someone might like a painting. Tell students they should review their answer(s) after the listening.

Preview Listening 2 Answer, p. 95
Answers will vary.

Listening 2 Background Note

Thomas Kinkade works primarily with oil paints. Oil paints have been a popular medium for paintings for hundreds of years, beginning in the 15th century in Europe. Famous paintings like *Milkmaid* and *Mona Lisa* were created with oil paints. Some artists prefer to work with oil because it doesn't dry quickly; therefore, the painting can be manipulated if an artist is unhappy with it.

Teaching Note

Students may find the following words/phrases difficult:

canvas: (noun) *a strong cloth that is used to paint on*

Henry Ford: (person) *inventor of the automobile and the assembly line*

pilgrimage: (noun) *a journey to a sacred place*

titan: (noun) *a person of great strength, size, or importance*

Cultural Note

The listening for this section includes the following line: *If you like six sugars in your coffee, these are the paintings for you.* This means that the paintings are pretty but may lack depth, and are enjoyed mostly for their "sweetness." Some might say they are *too* pretty.

LISTEN FOR MAIN IDEAS (10 minutes)

 CD2, Track 19

1. Preview the statements with students.
2. Play the audio and have students complete the activity individually.
3. Elicit the answers from the class. Ask students to explain why the false statements are not true.

Listen for Main Ideas Answers, p. 95
1. T;   **2.** F;   **3.** F;   **4.** F

 Listening and Speaking 4, page 96

LISTEN FOR DETAILS   (10 minutes)

 CD2, Track 20

1. Direct students to read the statements and answers before they listen again.
2. As you play the audio, have students choose the correct answer.
3. Have students compare answers with a partner.
4. Go over the answers with the class.

Listen for Details Answers, p. 96
1. c;   **2.** a;   **3.** a;   **4.** b

For additional practice with listening comprehension, have students visit *Q Online Practice*.

WHAT DO YOU THINK?

A (15 minutes)

1. Ask students to read the questions and reflect on their answers.
2. Seat students in small groups and assign roles: a group leader to make sure everyone contributes, a note-taker to record the group's ideas, a reporter to share the group's ideas with the class, and a timekeeper to watch the clock.
3. Give students ten minutes to discuss the questions. Call time if conversations are winding down. Allow extra time if necessary.
4. Call on each group's reporter to share ideas with the class.

Activity A Answers, p. 96
Answers will vary. Possible answers:
1. Thomas Kinkade creates paintings because he feels inspired to make art.
2. He has this goal because he wants to sell a lot of paintings and make a lot of money.

B (10 minutes)

1. Have students continue working in their small groups to discuss the questions in Activity B. Tell them to choose a new leader, note-taker, reporter, and timekeeper.
2. Call on the new reporter to share the group's answers to the questions.

Learning Outcome

Use the learning outcome to frame the purpose and relevance of Listenings 1 and 2. Ask: *What did you learn that prepares you to role-play a conversation expressing personal opinions about what makes art popular?* (Students' learned about two popular forms of art: manga and Thomas Kinkade paintings. They may want to use what they have learned in their role-plays.)

▶ *Listening and Speaking 4, page 97*

Vocabulary Skill: Word forms (15 minutes)

1. Present the information on word forms. Ask: *What other words do you know that have different forms?*

2. Check comprehension: *How does knowing word forms help you build your vocabulary? Where can you find different forms of a word?*

Skill Note

English learners often ask how a word can appear in one context and have one meaning and then appear in a different context and have a different meaning. Often, this is due to differences in word forms. When students learn new words, encourage them to find out if that word has other word forms.

Critical Thinking Tip (3 minutes)

1. Have a volunteer read the tip aloud.

2. Brainstorm some examples of when students need to distinguish information in the classroom and in daily life.

Critical Q: Expansion Activity

Distinguish

Choose 5–10 vocabulary words from this book that students have already studied. List each word with additional words forms on the board. For example, *identify*, *identification*, and *identifiable*.

Place students in pairs and have them distinguish between the different forms of the word. Encourage them to use a dictionary for help. Direct students to write sentences using some of the words or, as a challenge, include some of the words in a dialogue. Ask volunteers to read their sentences or perform their dialogues for the class.

A (10 minutes)

1. Go over number 1 as a class. Direct students to complete the activity individually. Have enough dictionaries on hand for students to use.

2. Go over the answers with the class.

Activity A Answers, p. 97
1. prodigy; **2.** perspire; **3.** deviate;
4. opera; **5.** ideally; **6.** marker

▶ *Listening and Speaking 4, page 98*

B (5 minutes)

1. Direct students to complete the sentences. Encourage students to use a dictionary for help.

2. Check the answers as a class.

Activity B Answers, p. 98
1. productive; **2.** inspiration; **3.** development;
4. operation; **5.** identifiable; **6.** marketable

Tip for Success (1 minute)

1. Ask a volunteer to read the tip aloud.

2. Ask: *Why is it important to learn how to pronounce the different word forms?* Remind students of words that have the same form but have different parts of speech and syllable stress. For example, *produce* (n.) vs. *produce* (v.); *project* (n.) vs. *project* (v.); *present* (n.) vs. *present* (v.).

 For additional practice with word forms, have students visit *Q Online Practice*.

▶ *Listening and Speaking 4, page 99*

SPEAKING

Grammar: Present perfect and present perfect continuous (30 minutes)

1. Divide the class into six groups. Assign three groups *present perfect* and three groups *present perfect continuous*.

2. Ask each group to read their section on page 99 to learn their specific grammar point with the intention of teaching that grammar point to others. Circulate around the room and answer questions as needed.

3. Pair up opposite groups and have them teach each other the grammar points.

4. Once the presentations have ended, review the information and examples in the skill box. Answer questions that students still have about these grammar points.

5. Check comprehension by asking questions: *When do we use the present perfect? When do we use the present perfect continuous? Can you give an example of each?* Elicit additional example sentences for the situations in which the tenses are used.

Skill Note

The present perfect and the present perfect continuous are tenses and aspects used to call specific attention to *when an action began* in relation to the present moment. So, when students ask, *How are these tenses different from simple past?* you can let them know that these tenses and aspects are concerned with when something began and when (or whether) it ended rather than just when it ended.

▶ *Listening and Speaking 4, page 100*

A (10 minutes)

1. Direct students to rewrite the sentences with the present perfect.

2. Put students in pairs to check their sentences.

3. Call on volunteers to share their sentences with the class. Discuss how the meaning of the sentence changes when the verb is changed to present perfect.

> **Activity A Answers, p. 100**
> **1.** Alonzo has started the project.
> **2.** I have thought a lot about going to art school.
> **3.** Ellen has taken several painting classes at the school.
> **4.** Min-ju has given several paintings to her mother.
> **5.** There have been several very good artists at my school.

Tip for Success (5 minutes)

1. Read the tip aloud.

2. Write the sentences on the board from Activity A but use contractions for *have* and *has*. Read each

sentence and have the class repeat. Then choose individual volunteers to repeat the sentence again.

B (15 minutes)

1. Have students work with a partner. Direct them to read the conversation and circle the correct verb forms.

2. Go over the answers with the class.

3. Call a volunteer to the front of the class to read through the conversation with you to model pronunciation.

4. Direct pairs to read the conversation together.

> **Activity B Answers, p. 100**
> **1.** have been going;   **2.** have seen;
> **3.** haven't gone;   **4.** haven't gone;
> **5.** have taken;   **6.** have been reading;
> **7.** have heard;   **8.** 've never seen

 For additional practice with the present perfect and present perfect continuous, have students visit *Q Online Practice*.

▶ *Listening and Speaking 4, page 101*

Pronunciation: Basic intonation patterns (15 minutes)

1. Present the pronunciation information and model the intonation in the examples. Ask: *Have you noticed how a person's voice goes up or down at the end of a sentence?*

2. Check comprehension by asking questions: *When do we use rising/falling intonation? When do we use rising intonation?*

Skill Note

Rising/falling intonation at the end of a sentence is the most common intonation pattern in English since it is used in statements, commands, and *wh-* questions. Rising intonation in *yes/no* questions indicates that the speaker is seeking a true answer. Sometimes rising intonation can be used with a full declarative sentence (*She's going where?*) or simply a phrase (*in the morning?*) to create a question.

A (10 minutes)

 CD2, Track 21

1. Preview the questions and statements and have students guess whether each will have rising or rising/falling intonation.

2. Play the audio. Direct students to mark their answers.

3. Review the answers as a class. Then have pairs practice the sentences.

> **Activity A Answers, p. 101**
> **1.** RF; **2.** R; **3.** RF; **4.** RF;
> **5.** R; **6.** RF; **7.** RF; **8.** R

▶ *Listening and Speaking 4, page 102*

B (10 minutes)
CD2, Track 22

1. Ask a volunteer to read the directions. Play the audio and stop it after the first sentence. Model how to draw arrows for the intonation pattern.

2. Play the audio again and have students complete the activity.

3. Review the answers as a class.

> **Activity B Answers, p. 102**
>
> Alex: Did you watch *Gravity* yet?
>
> Lee: Yeah, Jae and I watched it last weekend.
>
> Alex: What did you think of it?
>
> Lee: The special effects were great.
>
> Alex: That's it? Come on. Tell me what you thought.
>
> Lee: Well, the plot was ridiculous.
>
> I mean it was hard to believe.
>
> Alex: It's science fiction.
>
> It's not supposed to be realistic.
>
> Lee: I know. I guess sci fi isn't me.
>
> Jae thought it was pretty good. Did you like it?

 For additional practice with basic intonation patterns, have students visit *Q Online Practice*.

Speaking Skill: Avoiding answering questions (15 minutes)

1. Present the information on avoiding answering questions. Ask students in what situations they might want to avoid answering questions. Select pairs to read each conversation.

2. Check comprehension: *What are some ways to avoid answering a question? What are the most direct and least direct ways?*

▶ *Listening and Speaking 4, page 103*

A (10 minutes)
CD2, Track 23

1. Read the directions.

2. Play the audio and have students write the strategies.

3. Review the answers as a class. Have students explain how they chose the strategies they did.

4. Have pairs practice the conversations.

> **Activity A Answers, p. 103**
> **1.** Refuse politely.
> **2.** Ask another question.
> **3.** Ask another question.
> **4.** Answer a different question.
> **5.** Refuse politely.
> **6.** Ask another question.
> **7.** Ask another question.
> **8.** Use vague phrases.

▶ *Listening and Speaking 4, page 104*

B (10 minutes)

1. Read the directions and have students complete the task in pairs.

2. Have the pairs practice their questions and answers together. Choose a few pairs to read for the class.

> **Activity B Answers, p. 103**
> Answers will vary.

 For additional practice with avoiding answering questions, have students visit *Q Online Practice*.

Q Unit Assignment: Role-play a conversation about popular art

Unit Question (5 minutes)

Refer students back to the ideas they discussed at the beginning of the unit about what makes a work of art popular. Cue students if necessary by asking specific questions about the content of the unit: *What is art? Why do people like art? Why do you like art? What makes people want to buy art?* Read the direction lines for the assignment together to ensure understanding.

Learning Outcome

1. Tie the Unit Assignment to the unit learning outcome. Say: *The outcome for this unit is to role-play a conversation expressing personal opinions about what makes art popular. This Unit Assignment is going to let you practice your speaking and organizational skills by conducting a role-play. You will also be able to practice using the present perfect and present perfect continuous as well as correct intonation.*

2. Explain that you are going to use a rubric similar to their Self-Assessment checklist on p. 106 to grade their Unit Assignments. You can also share a copy of the Unit Assignment Rubric (on p. 56 of this *Teacher's Handbook*) with the students.

Consider the Ideas (15 minutes)

1. Put students into small groups and have them discuss their answers to the three questions.

2. Choose one person from each group to share their answers and reasons with the class.

▶ *Listening and Speaking 4, page 105*

Prepare and Speak

Gather Ideas

A (15 minutes)

1. Ask students to read the statements and select those that they agree with.

2. Choose a volunteer to read each statement. Designate one side of the classroom for agreeing with the statement and the other side for disagreeing with the statement. After each statement is read, have the students stand on the side of the room that matches their answer. Call on volunteers to give reasons for their choices.

Organize Ideas

B (20 minutes)

1. Ask a volunteer to read the directions for Activity B. Review the statements from Activity A.

2. Have students work in pairs to complete the activity. Tell students that they should look at their partner's answers for Activity A to complete number 2.

▶ *Listening and Speaking 4, page 106*

Speak

C (30–45 minutes)

1. Tell students to review the Self-Assessment checklist. Call on students to perform their role-play for the class.

2. Use the Unit Assignment Rubric on p. 56 of this *Teacher's Handbook* to score each student's presentation.

3. Alternatively, divide the class into two or three large groups and have pairs present their role-plays to their respective group. Have listeners complete the Unit Assignment Rubric, making sure there are enough copies for everyone.

Alternative Unit Assignments

Assign or have students choose one of these assignments to do instead of, or in addition to, the Unit Assignment.

1. Role-play an interview between an artist and a journalist. The journalist should ask questions about why the artist makes art.

2. Watch a movie that is currently popular. Then read a review of the movie. Tell the class why you agree or disagree with the review. Explain why you thought the movie was good or bad.

 For an additional Unit Assignment, have students visit *Q Online Practice*.

Check and Reflect

Check

A (10 minutes)

1. Direct students to read and complete the Self-Assessment checklist

2. Ask for a show of hands for how many students gave all or mostly *yes* answers. Congratulate them on their success.

3. Remind students that they can always refer to the checklist before they begin the Unit Assignment so they can focus on the skills they really need to complete the assignment successfully. Have students discuss with a partner what they can improve for next time.

B (10 minutes)

Have students consider the questions in pairs. When the conversations have died down, ask students to share something new that they learned. Ask: *How did your idea of what makes art popular change as we worked through the unit?*

▶ *Listening and Speaking 4, page 107*

Track Your Success (5 minutes)

1. Have students circle the words they have learned in this unit. Suggest that students go back through the unit to review any words they have forgotten.

2. Have students check the skills they have mastered. If students need more practice to feel confident about their proficiency in a skill, point out the page numbers and encourage them to review.

3. Read the learning outcome aloud *(Role-play a conversation expressing personal opinions about what makes art popular)*. Ask students if they feel that they have met the outcome.

Unit Assignment Rubric

Student name: _____

Date: _____

Unit Assignment: *Role-play a conversation about popular art.*

20 points = Role-play element was completely successful (at least 90% of the time).
15 points = Role-play element was mostly successful (at least 70% of the time).
10 points = Role-play element was partially successful (at least 50% of the time).
 0 points = Role-play element was not successful.

Role-play a Conversation	20 points	15 points	10 points	0 points
Student spoke easily and clearly about what makes art popular.				
Student adequately defended his or her opinions on popular art.				
Student used the present perfect and present perfect continuous correctly.				
Student used strategies to avoid answering questions.				
Student used correct intonation patterns.				

Total points: _____

Comments:

How has science changed the food we eat?

The Science of Food

LISTENING • understanding bias in a presentation
VOCABULARY • prefixes and suffixes
GRAMMAR • comparative forms of adjectives and adverbs
PRONUNCIATION • common intonation patterns
SPEAKING • expressing interest during a conversation

LEARNING OUTCOME

Participate in a debate on food science, stating and supporting your opinions about food modification.

▶ *Listening and Speaking 4, page 109*
Preview the Unit

Learning Outcome

1. Ask a volunteer to read the unit skills and then the unit learning outcome.

2. Explain: *This is what you are expected to be able to do by the unit's end. The learning outcome explains how you are going to be evaluated. With this outcome in mind, you should focus on learning these skills (Listening, Vocabulary, Grammar, Pronunciation, Speaking) that will support your goal of participating in a debate on food science, stating and supporting your opinions about food modification. This can also help you act as mentors in the classroom to help the other students meet this outcome.*

A (15 minutes)

1. Introduce the topic of food science. Ask: *How do you think science and food are connected?*

2. Put students in pairs or small groups to discuss the first two questions.

3. Call on volunteers to share their ideas with the class. Ask: *What influences your food choices the most? Do you know if you have ever eaten genetically modified food? Is genetically modified food better or worse than natural food? Why?*

4. Focus students' attention on the photo. Have a volunteer describe the photo to the class. Read the third question. Elicit students' answers. Ask: *Should science change natural foods in this way?*

Activity A Answers, p. 109
Answers will vary. Possible answers:

1. Cost is most important to me because I need to be careful about how much money I spend. / Taste is the most important thing because I like my food to taste good. / Nutrition is most important to me because I want to stay fit.

2. I know that scientists are trying to improve food with genetic modifications.

3. One of the tomatoes is purple. I think I might try it because maybe it tastes different or better.

B (15 minutes)

1. Introduce the Unit Question, *How has science changed the food we eat?* Ask related information questions or questions about personal experience to help students prepare for answering the more abstract Unit Question. Ask: *Do you think there are ways to make the food that we eat better? Do you grow any food at home? Are there ways to improve how we grow our food? Explain.*

2. Put students in small groups and give each group a piece of poster paper and a marker.

3. Read the Unit Question aloud. Give students a minute to silently consider their answers to the question. Tell students to pass the paper and marker around the group. Direct each group member to write a different answer to the question. Encourage them to help one another.

4. Ask each group to choose a reporter to read the answers to the class. Point out similarities and differences among the answers. Make a class list that incorporates all of the answers. Post the list to refer to later in the unit.

The Q Classroom

CD2, Track 24

1. Play The Q Classroom. Use the example from the audio to help students continue the conversation. Ask: *How did the students answer the question? Do you agree or disagree with their ideas? Why?*

2. Felix and Marcus state that packaged food is not healthy. Ask: *Do you agree? Why or why not?*

▶ *Listening and Speaking 4, page 110*

C (5 minutes)

Ask a volunteer to read the directions aloud. Then put students in groups to complete the activity.

D (10 minutes)

1. Place students in groups and direct them to discuss their choices.

2. Ask volunteers to share their answers with the class.

▶ *Listening and Speaking 4, page 111*

LISTENING

LISTENING 1: Food Additives Linked to Hyperactivity in Kids

VOCABULARY (25 minutes)

1. Direct students to read each sentence and try to guess what the word in bold means. Remind them to use context clues for help. Then they should write the word next to the correct definition.

2. Have students compare answers with a partner before eliciting the answers from volunteers. · Model the pronunciation of each word and have students repeat. Listen for correct syllable stress.

3. Write the vocabulary words on the board in two or three columns. Each column should include all the words. Divide the class into as many teams as there are columns and line up each team at an equal distance from the board.

4. When you read a definition, a member of each team at the front of the line should run up to the board and "slap" the word to which the definition refers. The fastest team gets a point. Then ask a student to use the word in a sentence.

5. Repeat for all the words.

> **MULTILEVEL OPTION**
>
> Group lower-level students and assist them with the task. Provide alternate example sentences to help them understand the words. For example, *Today is the **optimal** day for cleaning the yard because it isn't raining. I eat a **substantial** breakfast every morning.*

Vocabulary Answers, pp. 111–112

a. adverse;	**b.** artificial;	**c.** consist of;
d. consume;	**e.** identical;	**f.** optimal;
g. controversy;	**h.** significant;	**i.** substantial;
j. superfluous		

 For additional practice with the vocabulary, have students visit *Q Online Practice*.

▶ *Listening and Speaking 4, page 112*

PREVIEW LISTENING 1 (5 minutes)

1. Direct students to look at the photos. Ask: *How do you think science is connected to these two photos?*

2. Read the introduction aloud. Place students in mixed-ability pairs and have them discuss the question. Tell students they should review their answers after the listening.

Preview Listening 1 Answer, p. 112
Answers will vary.

Listening 1 Background Note

Two common food additives are artificial coloring and high-fructose corn syrup (HFCS). These additives are used to color and sweeten food. However, they have some side effects that are just now being studied. For example, HFCS can increase the risk of diabetes or obesity. Even though scientists are using additives to improve food longevity and taste, many people are considering the effects of additives on the human body and choosing to eat foods that do not have them.

LISTEN FOR MAIN IDEAS (10 minutes)

🔊 CD2, Track 25

1. Preview the statements with the students.

2. Play the audio and have students complete the activity individually.

3. Ask for volunteers to share their answers and the reasons why they chose those answers. Ask students to refer to specific parts of the audio track.

Listen for Main Ideas Answers, p. 112
Checked: Artificial additives can make young children hyperactive; Food coloring significantly affects the behavior of some children; The study is a source of controversy because some other studies do not have the same results; Feeding children heavily processed food is not optimal for health.

▶ *Listening and Speaking 4, page 113*

LISTEN FOR DETAILS (15 minutes)

🔊 CD2, Track 26

1. Direct students to read the directions and the statements before they listen again.

2. As you play the audio, have students write notes that support each statement.

3. Have students compare answers with a partner.

4. Replay the audio so that the partners can check their answers. Go over the answers with the class.

Listen for Details Answers, p. 113
Answers will vary. Possible answers:
1. ... effects are not just seen in children with extreme hyperactivity but can also be seen in the general population...
   Both mixtures significantly affected the older children, when compared with the regular drink.
2. Dr. Benjamin Feingold has written books arguing that not only do artificial colors, flavors, and preservatives affect children but so do natural chemicals found in some fruits and vegetables. Several studies have contradicted this notion. Some have only found an effect of food additives on the behavior of children diagnosed with extreme hyperactivity.

 For additional practice with listening comprehension, have students visit *Q Online Practice*.

❓ WHAT DO YOU THINK? (15 minutes)

1. Ask students to read the questions and reflect on their answers.

2. Seat students in small groups and assign roles: a group leader to make sure everyone contributes, a note-taker to record the group's ideas, a reporter to share the group's ideas with the class, and a timekeeper to watch the clock.

3. Give students ten minutes to discuss the questions. Call time if conversations are winding down. Allow them an extra minute or two if necessary.

4. Call on each group's reporter to share ideas with the class.

What Do You Think? Answers, p. 113
Answers will vary. Possible answers:
1. I am concerned about food additives, so I avoid food that isn't natural. I don't know what those chemicals can do.
2. I think food should decay over time. It's natural.
3. It is important that there are rules about food additives in food that kids eat because these chemicals can harm children more than other people.

Learning Outcome

Use the learning outcome to frame the purpose and relevance of Listening 1. Ask: *What did you learn from Listening 1 that prepares you to participate in a debate on food science, stating and supporting your opinions about food modification?* (Students learned about the effects of food additives on some children. These ideas may help them participate in their debate.)

▶ *Listening and Speaking 4, page 114*

Listening Skill: Understanding bias in a presentation (20 minutes)

1. Read the introductory information about bias. Then ask volunteers to read the information about each clue.

2. Check comprehension. *What is bias? What types of clues can help you understand bias in a presentation? How can an introduction help you find bias in a presentation? Why is the source of information for a presentation important when looking for bias?*

A (10 minutes)
🔊 CD2, Track 27

1. Direct students to read the directions and preview the clues.

2. Play the audio as students complete the activity. Then have students check their answers with a partner.

3. Elicit the answers from volunteers.

> **Activity A Answers, p. 114**
> **1.** title, introduction, imbalance; **2.** against

B (10 minutes)

 CD2, Track 28

1. Read the directions aloud and preview the statements.

2. Play the audio and have students circle their answers.

3. Go over answers as a class.

> **Activity B Answers, pp. 114–115**
> **1.** b; **2.** a; **3.** b; **4.** b

 For additional practice with understanding bias, have students visit *Q Online Practice*.

21ˢᵀ CENTURY SKILLS

Every day people are bombarded with messages on products, on the Internet, and in news reports. In order to decipher these messages, students have to analyze and evaluate evidence, arguments, claims, and beliefs. In short, students have to critically think about the source of each message and look for bias. Knowing how to identify bias will help students in both academic and professional settings to think about a person's message and their intentions behind it.

▶ *Listening and Speaking 4, page 115*
LISTENING 2: The "Flavr Savr" Tomato

VOCABULARY (15 minutes)

1. Direct students to read the vocabulary words and their definitions. Answer any questions about meaning and provide examples of the words in context.

2. Model the pronunciation of each word and have students repeat. Listen for correct syllable stress.

3. Ask students to complete each sentence with the correct vocabulary word and then compare answers with a partner.

4. Call on volunteers to read the sentences aloud.

MULTILEVEL OPTION

Group lower-level students and assist them with the task. Provide alternate example sentences to help them understand the words. For example, *The tailor **altered** the pants and made them shorter. The two candidates for president had a **debate** on television. One of Sara's best **traits** is her sense of humor.*

Ask higher-level students to write an additional sample sentence for each vocabulary word. Ask volunteers to write their sentences on the board. Correct the sentences as a class, focusing on the use of the words rather than other grammatical issues.

> **Vocabulary Answers, pp. 115–116**
> **1.** compound; **2.** hurdle; **3.** disturbing;
> **4.** consumer; **5.** reaction; **6.** alter;
> **7.** debate; **8.** trait; **9.** commodity;
> **10.** ultimate; **11.** ethics; **12.** modification

 For additional practice with the vocabulary, have students visit *Q Online Practice*.

▶ *Listening and Speaking 4, page 117*
PREVIEW LISTENING 2 (10 minutes)

1. Direct students' attention to the photo and ask: *Do you think science can make tomatoes better? Why or why not?*

2. Read the introduction aloud. Have students discuss their answers in pairs. Tell students they should review their answers after the listening.

> **Preview Listening 2, p. 117**
> Answers will vary.

Listening 2 Background Note

Biotechnology is a booming global business. Some companies focus on understanding the connection between genetics and health. Other companies produce genetically modified food such as corn and soy. There are also other "biotech" businesses that discover and sell new pharmaceutical products.

Teaching Note

Students may find the following words or phrases difficult:

agriculture: (noun) *the science or practice of farming*

biotechnology: (noun) *the manipulation of living organisms, such as plants, to produce more useful products*

blueprint: (noun) *the pattern in every living cell, which decides how the plant, animal or person will develop and what it will look like* human growth hormone: (noun) *a natural or genetically engineered hormone that is used to treat people with hormone deficiencies*

hybrid: (noun) *an animal or plant that has parents of different species or varieties*

insulin: (noun) *a chemical substance produced in the body that controls the amount of sugar in the blood*

organism: (noun) *a living thing, especially one that is extremely small*

LISTEN FOR MAIN IDEAS (10 minutes)

◀)) CD2, Track 29

1. Have students preview the statements and answer choices in pairs.
2. Play the audio and have students complete the activity individually.
3. Check answers as a class. Discuss the implications of these ideas. Ask: *How is biotechnology changing our world? Are the changes good, bad, or neutral? Do you support genetically modified foods? Why or why not?*

> **Listen for Main Ideas Answers, p. 117**
> **1.** a; **2.** c; **3.** b; **4.** b

LISTEN FOR DETAILS (10 minutes)

◀)) CD2, Track 30

1. Direct students to read the statements before they listen again.
2. Play the audio as students mark the statements *T* or *F.*
3. Have students compare answers with a partner. Replay the audio so that the partners can check their answers.
4. Go over the answers with the class. Elicit corrections for the false statements.

> **Listen for Details Answers, pp. 117–118**
> **1.** T; **2.** T; **3.** F; **4.** T; **5.** T

 For additional practice with listening comprehension, have students visit *Q Online Practice.*

▶ *Listening and Speaking 4, page 118*

WHAT DO YOU THINK?

A (15 minutes)

1. Ask students to read the questions and reflect on their answers.

2. Seat students in small groups and assign roles: a group leader to make sure everyone contributes, a note-taker to record the group's ideas, a reporter to share the group's ideas with the class, and a timekeeper to watch the clock.
3. Give students ten minutes to discuss the questions. Call time if conversations are winding down. Allow them an extra minute or two if necessary.
4. Call on each group's reporter to share ideas with the class.

> **Activity A Answers, p. 118**
> Answers will vary. Possible answers:
> **1.** Genetically modified foods can help feed a lot of people who are hungry, so I think the advantages outweigh the disadvantages.
> **2.** Consumers need information to make healthy choices, so we should label food that has been genetically modified. / I think that what customers don't know won't hurt them, so the items don't need be labeled.

B (10 minutes)

1. Have students continue working in their small groups to discuss the questions in Activity B. Tell them to choose a new leader, note-taker, reporter, and timekeeper.
2. Call on the new reporter to share the group's answers to the questions.

> **Activity B Answers, p. 118**
> Answers will vary. Possible answers.
> I know that genetically modified potatoes are used to make the potato chips I like. I'm thinking of giving up chips because of this information.

Learning Outcome

Use the learning outcome to frame the purpose and relevance of Listenings 1 and 2. Ask: *What did you learn that prepares you to participate in a debate on food science, stating and supporting your opinions about food modification?* (Students learned about additives and genetically modified foods. They may want to refer to these ideas in their debates.)

Vocabulary Skill: Prefixes and suffixes
(15 minutes)

1. Write a list of prefixes on the board: *pre-, un-, re-,* and *over-.* Ask students if they have seen words that start with these prefixes. Elicit examples of some words.

2. Next, write a list of suffixes on the board: -ion, -ness, -ly, and, -ist. Elicit examples of words with the suffixes.

3. Present the information on prefixes and suffixes. Ask volunteers to read each prefix/suffix, the meaning, and the example word.

4. Check comprehension: *What is a prefix? What is a suffix? What are some examples of both? What does* under- *mean? What does* –less *mean?*

Skill Note

Learning prefixes and suffixes is one way to expand students' vocabularies. By knowing what certain prefixes and suffixes mean, students can figure out the meanings of new words.

▶ *Listening and Speaking 4, page 119*

A (10 minutes)

1. Ask students to underline the main word in each item (e.g., dis*approve*).

2. Direct students to complete the activity individually.

3. Go over the answers with the class.

> **Activity A Answers, p. 119**
> **1.** not approve
> **2.** do again
> **3.** not fair
> **4.** not feed enough
> **5.** make loose
> **6.** not like

B (10 minutes)

1. Read the directions. Review the example together as a class.

2. Ask students to complete the activity individually. Then have students check their answers with a partner.

3. Check the answers as a class.

> **Activity B Answers, p. 119**
> **1.** scientist;   **2.** originally;   **3.** uniqueness;
> **4.** weightless;   **5.** topical;   **6.** relation

Tip for Success (1 minute)

1. Read the tip aloud.

2. Provide the words *science* and *relate* and ask students if they noticed which letter dropped when changing the word forms of both words. Ask: *Are there other words that lose letters when changing to a new form?*

EXPANSION ACTIVITY: You Know More Words Than You Thought! (15 minutes)

1. Write a paragraph that includes words with prefixes or suffixes. Alternatively, select a text from a book, magazine, or newspaper.

2. Distribute the text to students and place them in small groups of three.

3. Ask students to underline all of the words they think contain prefixes or suffixes. Then ask students to figure out what the suffixes or prefixes mean—along with the words themselves— without using a dictionary.

4. Allow students to use dictionaries to check their answers. Discuss the words and their meanings as a class. Point out how this activity helps strengthen their ability to figure out a word's meaning from context.

C (10 minutes)

1. Direct students to complete the activity individually.

2. Ask students to read their sentences to a partner. Ask a few volunteers to read their sentences to the class.

> **Activity C Answers, p. 119**
> Answers will vary.

 For additional practice with prefixes and suffixes, have students visit *Q Online Practice*.

SPEAKING

▶ *Listening and Speaking 4, page 120*

Grammar: Comparative forms of adjectives and adverbs (20 minutes)

1. Check for previous knowledge. Ask: *When have you seen comparative adjectives and adverbs before? When do we use them? Do you know or remember any rules for forming comparatives?*

2. Ask volunteers to read the information aloud. Stop them at logical points and provide additional information or examples as needed. Elicit additional examples from volunteers.

3. Check comprehension by asking: *What's the rule for forming comparatives from one-syllable adjectives or adverbs? Two-syllable adjectives that end in* –y? *How do you make* good *and* well *comparative? What word do you use to compare things or actions?*

Skill Note

Note the following common errors that English language learners may make with comparatives.

- Omitting the comparative ending: *Thailand is small than China.*

- Omitting the verb *be: Carlos shorter than Jun.*

- Using another word for *than: Carlos is shorter from Jun.*

- Using a regular comparative when an irregular form is needed: *My score was badder than his.*

- Using *more* instead of *–er: Carlos is more short than Jun.*

- Using a double comparative: *China is more bigger than Thailand.*

▶ *Listening and Speaking 4, page 121*

A (15 minutes)

1. Have a student read the directions for the activity aloud. Do item 1 as a class to model completing the task.

2. Have students write the comparative forms individually and then work with a partner to use the comparatives in sentences.

3. Go over the answers with the class. Call on volunteers to share some of their sentences.

Activity A Answers, p. 121
1. more flavorful
2. more uneasy
3. higher
4. tastier
5. more widely
6. more unnatural
7. more acceptable
8. worse
9. more loyal
10. more expensive

B (15 minutes)

1. Read the directions and example with the class. Ask students to think of other questions they could ask with the example words.

2. Direct students to complete the activity in pairs.

3. Elicit the questions and answers from volunteers.

Activity B Answers, p. 121
1. A: Which kind of juice is sweeter, pineapple or orange? B: I think (answer will vary) is sweeter than (answer will vary).
2. A: Which ice cream is tastier, chocolate or strawberry? B: I think (answer will vary) is tastier than (answer will vary).

3. A: Which TV show is more disturbing, the news or reality TV? B: I think (answer will vary) is more disturbing than (answer will vary).
4. A: Which drink is more widely enjoyed, tea or coffee? B: I think (answer will vary) is more widely enjoyed than (answer will vary).
5. A: Which food is more expensive, organic or genetically engineered? B: I think (answer will vary) is more expensive than (answer will vary).

 For additional practice with comparative forms of adjectives and adverbs, have students visit *Q Online Practice.*

▶ *Listening and Speaking 4, page 122*

Pronunciation: Other common intonation patterns (15 minutes)

CD2, Track 31

1. Present the information on common intonation patterns and play the audio as noted. Have students repeat the example sentences. Listen for correct intonation.

2. Check comprehension by asking questions: *In what situations do English speakers use specific intonation patterns? When do you use rising/falling intonation? How do you express surprise using intonation patterns?*

A (15 minutes)

CD2, Track 32

1. Direct students to preview the sentences and think about what intonation pattern might be used.

2. Play the audio as students mark the intonation patterns.

3. Put students in pairs to compare their answers. Then elicit the patterns from volunteers. Model the correct pattern for each sentence and have students repeat.

4. Have pairs practice saying the sentences.

Activity A Answers, p. 122

1. What? You've never eaten a tomato?

2. Do you prefer water or juice?

3. My favorite foods are rice, yams, and pizza

4. What did you say? You don't like ice cream?

5. Are you hungry?

Do you want some bread and cheese?

Listening and Speaking 4, page 123

B (10 minutes)

1. Ask a volunteer to read the directions. Read the questions aloud, using correct intonation patterns, and have students repeat.

2. Have students complete the activity in pairs. Circulate around the room and correct students' intonation as needed.

 For additional practice with other common intonation patterns, have students visit *Q Online Practice.*

Tip for Success (1 minute)

1. Read the tip aloud.

2. Explain to students that listening to native English speakers on the radio, television, or Internet will help them hear intonation patterns. Remind them that on the Internet, they can replay an audio clip to listen again to what the speaker said.

Speaking Skill: Expressing interest during a conversation (10 minutes)

1. Ask students: *How do you show someone that you are interested in what they are saying?* Write some of their ideas on the board.

2. Present the information about expressing interest. Model the words and phrases and have students repeat.

3. Check comprehension: *What are four ways people can express interest in a conversation?*

A (15 minutes)

CD2, Track 33

1. Have a volunteer read the directions aloud.

2. Play the audio and have students fill in the blanks.

3. Put students into pairs to compare answers.

4. Check the answers as a class. Then have students practice the conversation with a partner.

> **Activity A Answers, pp. 123–124**
> Marc: Really?; Wow;
> Noriko: Yeah!; Mm-hmm.; Every day!; That's interesting.

 Listening and Speaking 4, page 124

B (10 minutes)

1. Read the directions aloud. Place students into groups to discuss the questions. Check understanding: *What do you need to do as you discuss the questions?*

2. To help students remember to use the expressions, you may want to provide groups with a set of markers, such as paper clips or small coins. Each person gets the same number of markers. Every time a student uses an expression to show interest he or she can get rid of one marker.

 For additional practice with expressing interest during a conversation, have students visit *Q Online Practice.*

Unit Assignment: Express your opinion on an issue

Unit Question (5 minutes)

Refer students back to the ideas they discussed at the beginning of the unit about how science is changing the food that we eat. Pull out the lists from the Unit Question Activity B, completed at the beginning of the unit, and reflect on those answers. Cue students if necessary by asking specific questions about the content of the unit: *How is science changing food? How do people feel about these changes? How do you feel about these changes?* Read the directions for the assignment to ensure understanding.

Learning Outcome

1. Tie the Unit Assignment to the unit learning outcome. Say: *The outcome for this unit is to participate in a debate on food science, stating and supporting your opinions about food modification. This Unit Assignment is going to let you show your skill in expressing your opinion on an issue as well as using comparative adjectives and adverbs and expressing interest.*

2. Explain that you are going to use a rubric similar to their Self-Assessment checklist on p. 126 to grade their Unit Assignment. You can also share a copy of the Unit Assignment Rubric (on p. 67 of this *Teacher's Handbook*) with the students.

 Listening and Speaking 4, page 125

Critical Thinking Tip (3 minutes)

1. Read the Critical Thinking Tip aloud.

2. Ask the class why they think it is important to support their opinions with reasons.

Consider the Ideas (15 minutes)

1. Have students read the directions. Put students into groups and have them preview the photos.

2. Ask students to discuss the advantages and disadvantages of the situation each picture shows. Remind students to support their opinions.

3. Elicit ideas from volunteers.

Prepare and Speak

Gather Ideas

A (15 minutes)

1. Ask students to remain in their groups to complete this activity.

2. Once students have written their lists, have them work with new partners, from different groups, to share and explain their answers.

▶ *Listening and Speaking 4, page 126*

Organize Your Ideas

B (10 minutes)

Direct students to use the graphic organizer to organize their reasons and details.

Speak

C (30 minutes)

1. Quickly poll the class in order to divide them into two groups—one that supports genetically modified food and one that is against it. Using their notes from Activity B, students should be prepared to defend their side of the issue.

2. Pair up students from both groups. Call on each pair to debate the issue in front of the class, using their notes to support their opinions.

3. Use the Unit Assignment Rubric on p. 67 of this *Teacher's Handbook* to score each student's presentation.

4. Alternatively, divide the class into groups of six and have pairs debate in front of their groups. Have listeners complete the Unit Assignment Rubric as the pairs present their debates.

Alternative Unit Assignments

Assign or have students choose one of these assignments to do instead of, or in addition to, the Unit Assignment.

1. With a partner, create a survey listing several foods that commonly contain genetically modified ingredients and/or chemical additives. Then interview your classmates or people outside the classroom to find out if they would feel comfortable eating these foods.

2. Work in a small group. Have each group member choose a country and do online research on that country's position on genetically modified food. Find out if the government has any rules or laws about the genetically modified food that can be produced or imported. Compare your research results and decide if there are any similarities in the policies of these countries. Share your findings with the class.

 For an additional Unit Assignment, have students visit *Q Online Practice.*

Check and Reflect

Check

A (10 minutes)

1. Direct students to read and complete the Self-Assessment checklist.

2. Ask for a show of hands for how many students gave all or mostly *yes* answers. Congratulate them on their success.

3. Remind students that they can always refer to the checklist before they begin the Unit Assignment so they can focus on the skills they need to complete the assignment successfully. Have students discuss with a partner what they can improve for next time.

B (10 minutes)

Ask students to consider the questions in pairs. When the conversations have died down, ask students to share any new things they have learned. Ask: *How did your ideas about science and food change as we worked through the unit?*

▶ *Listening and Speaking 4, page 127*

Track Your Success (5 minutes)

1. Have students circle the words they have learned in this unit. Suggest that students go back through the unit to review any words they have forgotten.

2. Have students check the skills they have mastered. If students need more practice to feel confident about their proficiency in a skill, point out the page numbers and encourage them to review.

3. Read the learning outcome aloud (*Participate in a debate on food science, stating and supporting your opinions about food modification*). Ask students if they feel that they have met the outcome.

Unit 6   The Science of Food

Unit Assignment Rubric

Student name: _____

Date: _____

Unit Assignment: *Express your opinion on an issue.*

20 points = Presentation element was completely successful (at least 90% of the time).
15 points = Presentation element was mostly successful (at least 70% of the time).
10 points = Presentation element was partially successful (at least 50% of the time).
 0 points = Presentation element was not successful.

Express Your Opinion	20 points	15 points	10 points	0 points
Student expressed his or her opinions on genetically modified food.				
Student supported his or her opinions with reasons, details, or examples.				
Student used comparative adjectives and adverbs correctly.				
Student used intonation patterns correctly.				
Student used expressions to show interest.				

Total points: _____

Comments:

Unit QUESTION

Is one road to success better than another?

From School to Work

LISTENING • listening for contrasting ideas
VOCABULARY • synonyms for formality
GRAMMAR • simple, compound, and complex sentences
PRONUNCIATION • highlighted words
SPEAKING • changing the topic

LEARNING OUTCOME

Participate in a group discussion about people's job qualifications and arrive at a hiring decision.

▶ *Listening and Speaking 4, page 129*

Preview the Unit

Learning Outcome

1. Ask a volunteer to read the unit skills and then the unit learning outcome.

2. Explain: *This is what you are expected to be able to do by the unit's end. The learning outcome explains how you are going to be evaluated. With this outcome in mind, you should focus on learning these skills (Listening, Vocabulary, Grammar, Pronunciation, Speaking) that will support your goal of participating in a group decision about people's job qualifications and arrive at a hiring decision. This can also help you act as mentors in the classroom to help the other students meet this outcome.*

A (15 minutes)

1. Ask students about their life experiences: *What kind of success have you had in your life? How did you obtain that success? How do people find success in life?*

2. Put students in pairs or small groups to discuss the first two questions.

3. Call on volunteers to share their ideas with the class. Ask: *Who in your life is successful? What did they do to become successful?*

4. Focus students' attention on the photo. Have a volunteer describe the photo to the class. Read the third question aloud. Elicit students' answers.

> **Activity A Answers, p. 129**
> Answers will vary. Possible answers:
> **1.** Being successful means that I accomplish all of my personal goals.

2. I have taken a traditional path to success. I work hard, and I am going to school. The advantage to a traditional path is that it has worked for a lot of people for a long time. / I have taken a non-traditional path. I didn't go to school, and I didn't have good jobs when I was younger. However, I have become successful because I was given an opportunity later in life.

3. Maybe the person is advertising a comedy show that he or she is in. This person could become successful if the show is popular.

B (15 minutes)

1. Introduce the Unit Question, *Is one road to success better than another?* Explain the figurative meaning of the phrase "road to success." Ask related information questions or questions about personal experience to help students prepare for answering the more abstract Unit Question. Ask: *Is success something that everyone should try to obtain? Why or why not? What different ways are there to become successful?*

2. Read the Unit Question aloud. Give students a minute to silently consider their answers to the question. Then ask students who would answer *Yes, some roads are better* to stand on one side of the room and students who would answer *No, all roads are the same* to stand on the other side of the room.

3. Direct students to tell the person next to them their reasons for choosing the answer they did.

4. Call on volunteers from each side to share their opinions with the class.

5. After students have shared their opinions, provide an opportunity for anyone who would like to change sides to do so.

6. Ask students to sit down, copy the Unit Question, and make a note of their answers and their reasons. They will refer to these notes at the end of the unit.

> **Activity B Answers, p. 129**
> Answers will vary. Possible answers: Hard work is the best way to be successful. / Education is the best road to success because many people recognize the value of a college diploma. / No path to success is better than any other because success can happen to anyone at any time.

The Q Classroom

🔊 CD3, Track 2

1. Play The Q Classroom. Use the example from the audio to help students continue the conversation. Ask: *How did the students answer the question? Do you agree or disagree with their ideas? Why?*

2. Marcus says that he thinks it's better to take a non-traditional path to success. Ask: *What does he mean by* non-traditional? *Why would those paths be more helpful than traditional paths?*

▶ *Listening and Speaking 4, page 130*

C (15 minutes)

1. Ask a volunteer to read the directions aloud. Have students complete the questionnaire individually.

2. Put students in pairs to share their answers.

3. Call on students to share their answers with the class.

D (20 minutes)

1. Have students discuss the questions in groups of three.

2. Once they have done this, create new groups with one student from each original group. Have them share the answers from their first group.

3. After students have completed the activity, ask: *What ideas were different between your original groups and your new groups? Which were the same?*

LISTENING

▶ *Listening and Speaking 4, page 131*

LISTENING 1: Changing Ways to Climb the Ladder

VOCABULARY (15 minutes)

1. Direct students to read the vocabulary words and their definitions. Answer any questions about meaning and provide examples of the words in context.

2. Model the pronunciation of the words and have students repeat. Listen for correct syllable stress.

3. Direct students to complete the sentences with the vocabulary words. Call on volunteers to read the sentences aloud.

> **Vocabulary Answers, pp. 131–132**
> **1.** stable; **2.** devote; **3.** attitude;
> **4.** radically; **5.** counting on; **6.** model;
> **7.** currently; **8.** advancement; **9.** loyal;
> **10.** structure; **11.** career path; **12.** climb the ladder

---

MULTILEVEL OPTION

Group lower-level students and assist them with the task. Provide alternate example sentences to help them understand the words. Use these example sentences for more difficult vocabulary. For example, *The whole office is **counting on** you to do your work. One way to **climb the ladder** at work is to volunteer to do difficult tasks.*

Have higher-level students complete the activity individually and then compare answers with a partner. Tell the pairs to write an additional sentence for each word. Have volunteers write their sentences on the board. Correct the sentences with the whole class, focusing on the use of the words rather than grammatical issues.

 For additional practice with the vocabulary, have students visit *Q Online Practice*.

▶ *Listening and Speaking 4, page 132*

PREVIEW LISTENING 1 (5 minutes)

1. Direct students to look at the photo. Ask: *Does this picture show a symbol of success? Why or why not?*

2. Read the introduction aloud. Direct students to discuss the question with a partner.

> **Preview Listening 1 Answer, p. 132**
> Answers will vary.

Listening 1 Background Note

Often people work very hard to become successful. Li Ka-shing, a wealthy businessman from East Asia, started off life anything but rich and successful. In fact, he followed the second model mentioned in Listening 1—jumping from one business to another as he climbed the ladder. He left home in 1940 and settled in Hong Kong. At the age of 15, after a death in the family, Li Ka-shing began to work in a factory that manufactured plastic—having to leave school to do so. Later, he invested borrowed money into another plastics manufacturing venture which grew into a large business with interests in supermarkets and cell phones. Named one of the wealthiest people in the world, Li Ka-shing has often been seen wearing a $50 watch long after he became rich.

LISTEN FOR MAIN IDEAS (10 minutes)

◖◗ CD3, Track 3

1. Preview the statements with students.

2. Play the audio and have students complete the activity individually.

3. Ask volunteers to share their answers with the class. Elicit corrections for the false statements.

> **Listen for Main Ideas Answers, p. 132**
> **1.** T; **2.** F; **3.** F; **4.** T; **5.** T

▶ *Listening and Speaking 4, page 133*

LISTEN FOR DETAILS (15 minutes)

◖◗ CD3, Track 4

1. Direct students to read the statements in the chart before they listen again.

2. As you play the audio, have students check which model each statement represents.

3. Have students compare answers with a partner. Replay the audio if necessary.

4. Go over the answers with the class.

> **Listen for Details Answers, p. 133**
> **1.** traditional; **2.** new; **3.** new;
> **4.** traditional; **5.** traditional; **6.** new;
> **7.** traditional; **8.** new; **9.** new;
> **10.** new

 For additional practice with listening comprehension, have students visit *Q Online Practice*.

WHAT DO YOU THINK? (15 minutes)

1. Ask students to read the questions and reflect on their answers.

2. Seat students in small groups and assign roles: a group leader to make sure everyone contributes, a note-taker to record the group's ideas, a reporter to share the group's ideas with the class, and a timekeeper to watch the clock.

3. Give students ten minutes to discuss the questions. Call time if conversations are winding down. Allow extra time if necessary.

4. Call on each group's reporter to share ideas with the class.

> **What Do You Think? Answers, p. 133**
> Answers will vary. Possible answers:
> **1.** I think the traditional model fits me best. I'd like to work for a good company and stay there a long time. / I think the new model fits me best. I don't think one company can provide me with everything I want in my career.
> **2.** The traditional model works for laborers, professors, and doctors. The new model works for artists, writers, and entrepreneurs.

Learning Outcome

Use the learning outcome to frame the purpose and relevance of Listening 1. Ask: *What did you learn from Listening 1 that prepares you to participate in a group discussion about people's job qualifications and arrive at a hiring decision?* (Students learned about two different models of career advancement. They may want to refer to these models in their group discussion.)

▶ *Listening and Speaking 4, page 134*

Listening Skill: Listening for contrasting ideas (15 minutes)

1. Present the information on listening for contrasting ideas. Ask students to read the examples.

2. Provide practice with contrasting language. Write this sentence on the board: *Rather than go to college, Diego wants to work for a few years to gain new experiences.* Ask the class: *What words show you that there is a contrasting idea in this sentence?* (Answer: *rather than*). Provide a few more examples to highlight language that shows contrast: *Non-traditional paths to success are*

important. On the other hand, traditional methods have always worked. Staying with one company is easier than changing jobs.

3. Check comprehension: *What is a contrasting idea? What words can we use to signal contrasting ideas? Who can give me an example of a sentence that uses a contrasting idea?*

Tip for Success (1 minute)

1. Ask a volunteer to read the tip.

2. Ask students how they organize information when they speak. *What information is important to say first? In the middle? Last?*

A (10 minutes)

 CD3, Track 5

1. Direct students to read the directions.

2. Play the audio and have students fill in the blanks.

3. Have students compare answers with a partner.

4. Elicit the answers from the class. Direct students to practice the conversation in pairs.

> **Activity A Answers, p. 134**
> Mr. Doshi: whereas
> Ms. Stanz: but
> Mr. Doshi: However
> Ms. Stanz: On the other hand

B (10 minutes)

 CD3, Track 6

1. Read the directions aloud. Preview the chart with students.

2. Play the audio and have students complete the chart.

3. Check the answers as a class.

> **Activity B Answers, p. 135**
> Are employees loyal? Traditional (yes); New (no)
> Is the model like a family? Traditional (yes); New (no)
> Is it a single ladder model? Traditional (yes); New (no)
> Can workers advance quickly? Traditional (no); New (yes)
> Is the model more common today? Traditional (no); New (yes)

 For additional practice with listening for contrasting ideas, have students visit *Q Online Practice*.

▶ *Listening and Speaking 4, page 135*

LISTENING 2: Life Experience Before College

VOCABULARY (20 minutes)

1. Write the vocabulary words on the board and probe for prior knowledge. *What words do you already know? What do those words mean?*

2. Direct students to read each sentence and try to guess what the bold word means. Remind them to use context clues for help. Then they should write each word next to the correct definition.

3. Call on volunteers for the answers. Model the pronunciation of each word and have students repeat. Listen for correct syllable stress.

> **Vocabulary Answers, pp. 135–136**
> **a.** figure;   **b.** serve him well;   **c.** particular;
> **d.** peers;   **e.** log;   **f.** commute;
> **g.** stand out;   **h.** dare;   **i.** face;
> **j.** rigorous;   **k.** concept;   **l.** point

> **MULTILEVEL OPTION**
>
> Group lower-level students and assist them with the task. Provide alternate example sentences to help them understand the words. For example: *I wouldn't **dare** go out in the ocean. I'm not a good swimmer. The players were very tired after their **rigorous** practice. If you paint your house bright pink, it will **stand out** from all the others.*
>
> After higher-level students have completed the activity, ask pairs to write an additional sentence for each word. Have volunteers write their sentences on the board. Correct the sentences as a class, focusing on the use of the words rather than other grammatical issues.

 For additional practice with the vocabulary, have students visit *Q Online Practice*.

▶ *Listening and Speaking 4, page 136*

PREVIEW LISTENING 2 (10 minutes)

1. Direct students' attention to the photo and ask: *What do you think of when you see a backpack like this? When do people use these kinds of backpacks? How do you think these backpacks relate to life before college?*

2. Read the introduction aloud. Direct students to discuss the question with a partner. Tell students they should review their answers after the listening.

Preview Listening 2 Answer, p. 136
Answers will vary.

Listening 2 Background Note

One "gap-year" option for American students is AmeriCorps. AmeriCorps is a U.S. program that matches volunteers with communities that are in need of aid in fields such as education, disaster relief, community development, and homelessness. The commitment is only ten months, which makes AmeriCorps a popular option for people who want real world experience before heading off to college.

Teaching Note

Students may find the following words or phrases difficult.

academia: (noun) *the academic life, community, or world*

better off: (idiom) *used to say that someone would be happier or more satisfied if they were in a particular position or doing a particular thing*

community service: (noun) *work helping people in the local community that someone does without being paid*

dive into: (phrasal verb) *to start doing something fully, with a lot of energy and enthusiasm*

globetrotting: (adj) *traveling in many countries all over the world*

grant: (noun) *a sum of money that is given an organization to be used for a particular purpose*

international relations : (noun) *a branch of political science concerned with relationships between nations*

slacker: (noun) *a person who is lazy and avoids work*

21ST CENTURY SKILLS

Employers and schools value individuals with unique experiences, especially when the experiences involve helping one's community.

Civic literacy is a crucial 21st century skill. Discuss with students how they can get involved and help in their community. Ask: *How can you combine your goals with the betterment of your community? What opportunities are there in your local area for civic engagement?* Have students brainstorm ideas and consider doing a short class project where people can get involved in their communities.

▶ *Listening and Speaking 4, page 137*

LISTEN FOR MAIN IDEAS (15 minutes)

)) CD3, Track 7

1. Preview the statements with the students.
2. Play the audio and have students complete the activity individually.
3. Call on volunteers for the answers. Elicit corrections for the false statements.

Listen for Main Ideas Answers, p. 137
1. F; **2.** T; **3.** T; **4.** F; **5.** T

LISTEN FOR DETAILS (10 minutes)

)) CD3, Track 8

1. Direct students to read the statements and possible answers before they listen again.
2. As you play the audio, have students listen and circle their answers.
3. Have students compare answers with a partner.
4. Replay the audio so partners can check their answers. Elicit the answers from volunteers.

Listen for Details Answers, p. 137
1. a; **2.** c; **3.** b; **4.** c; **5.** b

 For additional practice with listening comprehension, have students visit *Q Online Practice.*

▶ *Listening and Speaking 4, page 138*

WHAT DO YOU THINK?

A (15 minutes)

1. Ask students to read the questions and reflect on their answers.
2. Seat students in small groups and assign roles: a group leader to make sure everyone contributes, a note-taker to record the group's ideas, a reporter to share the group's ideas with the class, and a timekeeper to watch the clock.
3. Give students ten minutes to discuss the questions. Call time if conversations are winding down. Allow them an extra minute or two if necessary.
4. Call on each group's reporter to share ideas with the class.

Activity A Answers, p. 138

Answers will vary. Possible answers:

1. I would go to Thailand and help some of the people in the north.
2. I would tell my friend to make a plan in order to make the most of the year off.
3. Volunteering to teach children or adults how to read could prepare someone for a career in education. If a person served as the treasurer of an organization, this experience could help him or her learn more about banking.

B (10 minutes)

1. Have students continue working in their small groups to discuss the questions in Activity B. Tell them to choose a new leader, note-taker, reporter, and timekeeper.
2. Call on the new reporter to share the group's answers to the questions.

Activity B Answers, p. 138

Answers will vary. Possible answers:

1. I've chosen a traditional path. I probably did this because that's what most people do in my country.
2. I wanted to wait a year before I started college, but if you do that, it's actually harder to get into a university later.

Learning Outcome

Use the learning outcome to frame the purpose and relevance of Listenings 1 and 2. Ask: *What did you learn that prepares you to participate in a group discussion about people's job qualifications and arrive at a hiring decision?* (Students learned about traditional and non-traditional paths to working and going to college. These ideas may help them during their discussion.)

Vocabulary Skill: Using the dictionary

(15 minutes)

1. Probe for previous knowledge. Ask: *What's the difference between formal and more casual language?* Elicit any examples students know.
2. Present the skill. If possible, have students look at their dictionaries during the presentation when appropriate.
3. Check comprehension: *How can using the dictionary help you find differences between formal and informal language?*

Skill Note

Knowing informal language can help students to talk like a native speaker. However, it is important to raise students' awareness of when it is appropriate to use certain formal words and phrases versus informal language such as phrasal verbs and idioms.

MULTILEVEL OPTION

Have higher-level student volunteers role-play a conversation for making a request at work or school using formal language. One person is the manager (or teacher) and the other is the employee (or student). Then have the volunteers role-play a similar conversation using casual language. Have lower-level students report examples of the formal and casual language used in the role-play. Ask if the role-play with casual language would actually be appropriate with a real teacher or manager.

▶ *Listening and Speaking 4, page 139*

A (5 minutes)

1. Direct students to work with a partner to check the more formal sentences.
2. Go over the answers with the class.

Activity A Answers, p. 139
1. b; 2. a; 3. a; 4. b

B (10 minutes)

1. Direct students to complete the activity individually and then check their answers with a partner.
2. Check the answers as a class. Ask students if (or where) they've heard these words before.

Activity B Answers, pp. 139–140
1. a; 2. b; 3. a; 4. c; 5. b; 6. b

▶ *Listening and Speaking 4, page 140*

C (10 minutes)

1. Direct students to look at the photo. Ask: *Is this a formal or informal situation?*
2. Ask students to read the conversation and circle the appropriate synonyms.
3. Elicit the answers from the class.
4. Ask students to practice the conversation with a partner.

Activity C Answers, p. 140
speak; wait; begin; interested in

 For additional practice with formal and less formal language, have students visit *Q Online Practice*.

SPEAKING

Grammar: Simple, compound, and complex sentences (20 minutes)

1. Present the information on simple, compound, and complex sentences. Answer questions as they arise. Provide additional examples of each type of sentence.

2. Check comprehension by asking questions: *What is a simple sentence? How is a compound sentence different from a complex sentence? What are the pieces of a complex sentence? What comes at the beginning of a dependent clause? Why is it important to know the difference between these types of sentences?*

Skill Note

Here are some additional notes about these three types of sentences.

- A simple sentence contains at least one subject and one verb.

- In a compound sentence, each clause has equal importance.

- Both coordinating and subordinating conjunctions help specify the relationship between the two clauses in a sentence.

Subordinating conjunctions fall into categories, such as:

Time: *after, as soon as, before, when, whenever*

Reason: *because, since*

Purpose: *so*

Simultaneous: *while*

Conditional: *if, even if, as long as*

Concessive: *although, even though, though*

EXPANSION ACTIVITY: Round Robin
Sentence Writing (15 minutes)

1. Take three slips of paper and write *simple*, *compound*, and *complex*—one word on each piece.

2. Place students into groups of three.

3. Draw a slip of paper and read it to the class. Then each group has to write that type of sentence.

4. Have a volunteer from each group write their sentence on the board.

5. Discuss the sentences as a class and elicit corrections as needed. Continue until students are writing the sentences correctly most of the time.

A (10 minutes)

1. Direct students to complete the activity individually.

2. Put students in pairs to compare their answers. Have them support their choices with the information from the skill box.

3. Elicit the answers from volunteers.

> **Activity A Answers, pp. 141–142**
> **1.** simple; **2.** compound; **3.** complex;
> **4.** simple; **5.** complex

B (10 minutes)

1. Read the directions and combine the first two sentences as a class.

2. Ask students to complete this activity by rewriting the sentences in their notebooks.

3. Check the answers as a class. Have partners practice the conversation.

> **Activity B Answers, p. 142**
> Sam: Hi! It went really well, **and** I might get the job!
> Sam: **After** they make the decision this afternoon, they'll call me.
> Sam: No. I sent her an email last week, **but** she hasn't answered it.
> Inez: Well, **because** she's taking a year off to study penguins, she's going to Antarctica.
> Inez: Yeah. It seems like an incredible opportunity, **although** I can't imagine living in Antarctica.
> Inez: I might volunteer for a group that builds houses for poor people, **or** I might work in a program for street kids.
> Sam: Those both sound like good causes, **and** they'll look good on your college application.
> Inez: Yeah. I need to do something big **if** I want to get into a good school!
> Sam: Well, I should get home **so** I can wait for the call about the job.

 For additional practice with simple, compound, and complex sentences, have students visit *Q Online Practice*.

▶ Listening and Speaking 4, page 143

Pronunciation: Highlighted words (10 minutes)

🔊 CD3, Track 9

1. Probe for prior knowledge by asking: *Have you ever noticed when someone is speaking that some words will be louder or have longer sounds than others? Why do you think that happens? How do you change your speech when you want to emphasize a point or piece of information?*

2. Present the information on highlighted words and play the audio when noted. Ask volunteers to read the examples, and make sure that they stress the highlighted words.

3. Check comprehension by asking questions: *What's a highlighted word? Why do speakers use them? Should every word in a sentence be highlighted? Why not?*

4. Read some of the sentences from the conversation on page 142, highlighting certain words. Ask volunteers to do the same. Discuss what is being communicated or emphasized.

A (10 minutes)

🔊 CD3, Track 10

1. Direct students to preview the questions and think about what words might be highlighted.

2. Play the audio and have students complete the activity.

3. Put students in pairs to compare answers.

4. Call on volunteers to read the sentences. Have students practice with a partner.

> **Activity A Answers, p. 143**
> **1.** love; **2.** one; **3.** Carlos;
> **4.** not; **5.** lot; so

B (10 minutes)

🔊 CD3, Track 11

1. Ask a volunteer to read the directions. Direct students to preview the sentences and answers.

2. Play the audio. Have students complete the activity individually.

3. Review the answers as a class and elicit or offer corrections as needed.

> **Activity B Answers, pp. 143–144**
> **1.** c; **2.** a; **3.** b; **4.** a; **5.** c

▶ Listening and Speaking 4, page 144

C (10 minutes)

1. Place students into pairs and have them practice the conversation.

2. Ask for volunteers or choose a pair whose skill with the conversation you like. Ask them to read the conversation for the class. Point out the positive aspects of their conversation (e.g., *She really emphasizes the highlighted words; He pauses around each highlighted word*).

 For additional practice with highlighted words, have students visit *Q Online Practice*.

Speaking Skill: Changing the topic (10 minutes)

1. Ask volunteers to read the text aloud. Stop them at logical points and provide additional information or examples as needed.

2. Ask: *When have you had to change the topic in a conversation before? Why is it a useful skill?*

3. Check comprehension. Ask: *What's something that you want to avoid when changing the topic? What are some phrases we can use to change the topic politely? What can you say when you want to mention something about an unrelated topic? What can you say to return to the previous topic?*

▶ Listening and Speaking 4, page 145

A (15 minutes)

🔊 CD3, Track 12

1. Have a volunteer read the directions aloud.

2. Play the audio and have students fill in the blanks.

3. Put students into pairs to compare answers. Check the answers as a class.

4. Have students practice the conversation.

> **Activity A Answers, pp. 145–146**
> That reminds me; I wanted to ask you; Anyway; Speaking of which; Hold that thought

▶ Listening and Speaking 4, page 146

B (15 minutes)

1. Place students into groups of three or four and have them read the directions for the activity.

2. Have students discuss the questions in their groups. Circulate around the room to ensure everyone is getting a chance to "change the topic" from what is being said.

3. Ask volunteers to discuss one of the questions in front of the class.

 For additional practice with changing the topic, have students visit *Q Online Practice*.

Unit Assignment:
Reach a group decision

Unit Question (5 minutes)

Refer students back to the ideas they discussed at the beginning of the unit about if one road to success is better than another. Ask students to take out their notes that they took from Activity B at the beginning of the unit. Cue students if necessary by asking specific questions about the content of the unit: *What are some traditional paths to success? What are some non-traditional paths? What do some people like to do before going off to college? Is there only one way to become successful? Why or why not?* Read through the directions to ensure understanding of the assignment.

Learning Outcome

1. Tie the Unit Assignment to the unit learning outcome. Say: *The outcome for this unit is to participate in a group discussion about people's job qualifications and arrive at a hiring decision. This Unit Assignment is going to let you show your skill in reaching a group decision as well as changing the topic and emphasizing highlighted words.*

2. Explain that you are going to use a rubric similar to their Self-Assessment checklist on p. 148 to grade their Unit Assignment. Ask students to read the checklist so they have a clear understanding of how they will be assessed.

Consider the Ideas (20 minutes)

 CD3, Track 13

1. Direct students to read the advertisement. Answer any vocabulary questions about the ad.

2. When students have finished reading, ask: *Who placed this job ad? Who are they looking for? What qualifications must applicants have?*

3. Have students read the information about the applicants on page 147. Ask: *Who do you think is right for this job?*

4. Play the audio. Ask students to take notes as they listen. Have students compare notes with a partner. Elicit notes from volunteers.

Consider the Ideas Answers, p. 147
Answers will vary. Possible answers:
Susan Jones: housewife; wants to come back to U.S. to be close to family; wants to help students have new experiences; speaks Spanish, Polish, and a little Thai
Doug Orman: wanted a promotion, but didn't get it; wants a career change; a lot of travel experience; studied Russian and French; doesn't speak either fluently
Narayan Tej: just finished college; from India; would bring multi-cultural aspect to team; has traveled a lot; speaks English and Hindi and a little Spanish and French
Teresa Lopez: took a gap year; wants to help students; speaks no other languages

Teaching Note

In the listening for Consider the Ideas, Susan Jones says that her son has had a baby. This means that his spouse just gave birth to their child.

▶ *Listening and Speaking 4, page 147*

Prepare and Speak

Gather Ideas

A (5 minutes)

1. Say: *Now that you've listened to their personal statements, have your thoughts on who would be good for the job changed?*

2. Direct students to rank their choices individually.

▶ *Listening and Speaking 4, page 148*

Organize Ideas

B (10 minutes)

1. Based upon their rankings in Activity A, ask students to expand upon their ideas and explain, in writing, why they ranked each candidate the way that they did.

2. Make sure that students rely on facts from the applicants' statements or resumes. Discourage students from focusing on information such as gender and age.

Critical Thinking Tip (3 minutes)

1. Ask a volunteer to read the tip aloud.

2. Brainstorm with students when they have had to rank information.

Speak

C (30 minutes)

1. Have students practice sharing their opinions with a partner before speaking in a group. Students should be prepared to discuss their choice and provide reasons that show they have thought carefully about the information.

2. Ask students to share their rankings and reasons with their group. Remind students that each group has to choose one person to hire and explain how they came to their decision. Encourage students to reach a consensus and be ready to share their choice with the class.

3. Use the Unit Assignment Rubric on p. 78 of this *Teacher's Handbook* to score each student's performance. You can also share a copy of the Unit Assignment Rubric with the students.

4. Have each group share with the class who they chose to hire and why.

Alternative Unit Assignments

Assign or have students choose one of these assignments to do instead of, or in addition to, the Unit Assignment.

1. These jobs are all considered stressful. What would be stressful about working in these jobs? What type of person is best suited for each job?

air traffic controller	journalist
medical doctor	customer service
stockbroker	employee
police officer	server in a busy
teacher	restaurant

2. Prepare a presentation about someone who has a successful career. Do online research as necessary to gather information. Prepare a time line to show the significant steps the person took to climb the ladder. Consider the best road to success. Present your findings to your classmates.

 For an additional Unit Assignment, have students visit *Q Online Practice*.

Check and Reflect

Check

A (10 minutes)

1. Direct students to read and complete the Self-Assessment checklist.

2. Ask for a show of hands for how many students gave all or mostly *yes* answers. Congratulate them on their success.

3. Remind students that they can always refer to the checklist before they begin the Unit Assignment so they can focus on the skills they really need to complete the assignment successfully. Have students discuss with a partner what they can improve for next time.

Reflect

B (10 minutes)

Ask students to consider the questions in pairs. When the conversations have died down, have students share something new that they have learned. Ask: *How did your ideas about roads to success change as we worked through this unit?*

▶ *Listening and Speaking 4, page 149*

Track Your Success (5 minutes)

1. Have students circle the words they have learned in this unit. Suggest that students go back through the unit to review any words they have forgotten.

2. Have students check the skills they have mastered. If students need more practice to feel confident about their proficiency in a skill, point out the page numbers and encourage them to review.

3. Read the learning outcome aloud (*Participate in a group discussion about people's job qualifications and arrive at a hiring decision*). Ask students if they feel that they have met the outcome.

Unit Assignment Rubric

Student name: _____

Date: _____

Unit Assignment: *Reach a group decision.*

20 points = Discussion element was completely successful (at least 90% of the time).
15 points = Discussion element was mostly successful (at least 70% of the time).
10 points = Discussion element was partially successful (at least 50% of the time).
 0 points = Discussion element was not successful.

Reach a Group Decision	20 points	15 points	10 points	0 points
Student spoke easily and clearly about the job candidates.				
Student gave strong reasons for his or her choice.				
Student correctly used vocabulary from the unit.				
Student used phrases to add to the topic.				
Student emphasized specific words to convey a particular message.				

Total points: _____

Comments:

Unit QUESTION
How can chance discoveries affect our lives?

Discovery

LISTENING • listening for signal words and phrases
VOCABULARY • collocations with prepositions
GRAMMAR • indirect speech
PRONUNCIATION • linked words with vowels
SPEAKING • using questions to maintain listener interest

LEARNING OUTCOME

Recount the events involved in a personal discovery you made accidently and tell how it affected you.

▶ *Listening and Speaking 4, page 151*
Preview the Unit

Learning Outcome

1. Ask a volunteer to read the unit skills and then the unit learning outcome.

2. Explain: *This is what you are expected to be able to do by the unit's end. The learning outcome explains how you are going to be evaluated. With this outcome in mind, you should focus on learning these skills (Listening, Vocabulary, Grammar, Pronunciation, Speaking) that will support your goal of recounting the events involved in a personal discovery you made accidently and tell how it affected you. This can also help you act as mentors in the classroom to help the other students meet this outcome.*

A (15 minutes)

1. Ask: *What's a discovery? What important discoveries have been made in the world?*

2. Put students in pairs or small groups to discuss the first two questions.

3. Call on volunteers to share their ideas with the class. Ask: *Why are discoveries important? What recent discoveries have improved modern life? Why?*

4. Focus students' attention on the photo. Ask a volunteer to describe the photo. Read the third question aloud. Elicit students' answers.

Activity A Answers, p. 151
Answers will vary. Possible answers:
1. He probably meant that a lot of his knowledge comes from things that he was not looking for.

2. I once accidentally added the wrong ingredient to a dish. I thought it would ruin the dish, but it ended up tasting great!
3. The man is digging for fossils. He has found a fossil of a shell.

B (15 minutes)

1. Introduce the Unit Question, *How can chance discoveries affect our lives?* Ask related information questions or questions about personal experience to help students prepare for answering the more abstract Unit Question: *What is a* chance *discovery? Which important discoveries do you think were made by accident? How do discoveries affect people?*

2. Read the Unit Question aloud. Point out that answers to the questions can fall into categories (e.g., make life easier, improve our knowledge, keep people healthy, improve our society). Give students a minute to silently consider their answers to the question and categories under which their answers could fall.

3. With the students, decide on three or four categories to use. Write each category at the top of a sheet of poster paper. Have students consider specific discoveries that fall into the categories. Make notes under the correct heading. Post the lists to refer to later in the unit.

Activity B Answers, p. 151
Answers will vary. Possible answers: These kinds of discoveries can improve our lives. / Usually, discoveries make life better or easier, and chance discoveries make our lives better in ways we weren't looking for. / Chance discoveries may distract us from the things that we were trying to look for.

The Q Classroom

 CD3, Track 14

1. Play The Q Classroom. Use the example from the audio to help students continue the conversation. Ask: *How did the students answer the question? Do you agree or disagree with their ideas? Why?*

2. In the audio, each of the students talks about chance discoveries in very positive ways. Ask: *Do you think there are some situations where chance discoveries aren't always so positive? If so, in what situations?*

▶ *Listening and Speaking 4, page 152*

C (10 minutes)

1. Ask a volunteer to read the directions.

2. Direct students to complete the task. Place students into pairs and ask them to share their answers. Ask: *Which choices did you both consider to have had the greatest effect on the world? Why? Why didn't you choose the other options?*

D (10 minutes)

1. Ask a volunteer to read the question aloud. Have students write their answers in their notebooks.

2. Put students into pairs and have them discuss their responses.

3. Elicit responses from the class

▶ *Listening and Speaking 4, page 153*

LISTENING

LISTENING 1:
The Power of Serendipity

VOCABULARY (15 minutes)

1. Direct students to read each sentence and try to guess what the word in bold means. Remind them to use context clues for help. Then have students circle the best answer.

2. Put students in pairs to compare answers.

3. Elicit the answers from volunteers. Model the pronunciation of each word and have students repeat. Listen for correct syllable stress.

4. Ask questions to help students connect with the vocabulary: *Do you know anyone who is **unreliable**? Have you ever **inadvertently** done something good? What things in your lives are **mandatory**?*

Vocabulary Answers, pp. 153–154
1. b; **2.** a; **3.** a; **4.** a; **5.** a; **6.** b;
7. a; **8.** b; **9.** b; **10.** b; **11.** b; **12.** a

MULTILEVEL OPTION

Have higher-level students write an additional sentence for each word. Have volunteers write their sentences on the board. Correct the sentences with the whole class, focusing on the use of the words rather than other grammatical issues.

For additional practice with the vocabulary, have students visit *Q Online Practice*.

▶ *Listening and Speaking 4, page 154*

PREVIEW LISTENING 1 (5 minutes)

1. Direct students to read the introduction and discuss the question with a partner.

2. Tell students they should review their answers after listening to the audio.

Preview Listening 1 Answer, p. 154
Answers will vary.

Listening 1 Background Note

Alfred Nobel not only discovered dynamite—the Nobel Prize is also named for him. The line in the listening, *Nothing like starting off with a bang,* refers to the bang that dynamite makes when it is set off.

Teaching Note

Note the following language from the listening that may be difficult for students. The phrase *aka* means "also known as." The listening refers to *GE*, which stands for the large company General Electric. The phrase *white glove treatment* means that something is treated as if it is delicate and special.

▶ *Listening and Speaking 4, page 155*

LISTEN FOR MAIN IDEAS (10 minutes)

CD3, Track 15

1. Read the directions as a class. Have students preview the statements.

2. Play the audio and ask students to complete the activity individually.

3. Discuss the answers as a class. Ask volunteers to explain why they chose their answers. Elicit corrections for the false statements.

Listen for Main Ideas Answers, p. 155
1. T; **2.** F; **3.** F; **4.** T; **5.** F

LISTEN FOR DETAILS (5 minutes)

 CD3, Track 16

1. Have students preview the activity.

2. Play the audio and direct students to write the best letter for each event.

3. Have students compare answers with a partner.

4. Play the audio again if necessary.

5. Go over the answers with the class.

Listen for Details Answers, p. 155
1. d; **2.** b; **3.** a; **4.** c; **5.** f; **6.** e

 For additional practice with listening comprehension, have students visit *Q Online Practice*.

▶ *Listening and Speaking 4, page 156*
WHAT DO YOU THINK? (20 minutes)

1. Ask students to read the questions and reflect on their answers.

2. Seat students in small groups and assign roles: a group leader to make sure everyone contributes, a note-taker to record the group's ideas, a reporter to share the group's ideas with the class, and a timekeeper to watch the clock.

3. Give students ten minutes to discuss the questions. Call time if conversations are winding down. Allow them an extra minute or two if necessary.

4. Call on each group's reporter to share ideas with the class.

What Do You Think? Answers, p. 156
Answers will vary. Possible answers:
1. I think that serendipity is a matter of chance.
2. Companies are smart to invest in research because if an important discovery is made by chance, the company will be able to make a lot of money. / Companies should not invest in research because they shouldn't risk money on a chance that something good might happen.
3. I do not think that serendipity is mandatory because it is a naturally occurring event. Not all naturally occurring events must happen to everyone. / I think serendipity is mandatory because it is hard to accomplish things without some element of chance.

Learning Outcome

Use the learning outcome to frame the purpose and relevance of Listening 1. Ask: *What did you learn from Listening 1 that prepares you to recount the events involved in a personal discovery you made accidentally and tell how it affected you?* (Students learned about some important products that were discovered by chance. They may want to refer to these products in their stories about personal discoveries.)

Listening Skill: Listening for signal words and phrases (10 minutes)

1. Go over the information in the skill box. Have students brainstorm situations in which listening for signal words and phrases can be extremely helpful—for example, at work when a boss explains something or in the classroom when the teacher introduces new information.

2. Check comprehension. Ask: *What words can you listen for that act as signals? What words do speakers use when they are about to provide an explanation?*

EXPANSION ACTIVITY:
Use Signal Words and Phrases (15 minutes)

1. Place students into pairs. Assign each the role of either speaker or listener.

2. Choose current events that students can discuss knowledgeably. Have the speaker talk about one of the topics and use signal words and phrases. (e.g., *Water on Mars is an important discovery. What I mean by this is that if there is water on Mars, there might be life on Mars.*)

3. Have the listener note all of the signal words and phrases that the speaker uses.

4. After five minutes, have partners switch roles and talk about a new topic. Circulate around the room to ensure that students are using signal words and phrases as they speak.

▶ *Listening and Speaking 4, page 157*
A (10 minutes)
 CD3, Track 17

1. Ask a volunteer to read the directions.

2. Play the audio and direct students to fill in the blanks with signal words and phrases.

3. Discuss and check answers as a class.

Activity A Answers, p. 157
which is; what is; In other words; In other words; I mean

B (10 minutes)

1. Ask a volunteer to read the directions.

2. After the students have written their answers, have them read the sentences with a partner.

3. Elicit the answers from volunteers.

> **Activity B Answers, pp. 157–158**
> Answers will vary. Possible answers:
> **1.** What I mean is
> **2.** In other words
> **3.** What I mean is
> **4.** In other words / This means
> **5.** This means

 For additional practice with listening for signal words and phrases, have students visit *Q Online Practice.*

▶ *Listening and Speaking 4, page 158*

LISTENING 2:
Against All Odds, Twin Girls United

VOCABULARY (20 minutes)

1. Direct students to read the vocabulary words and definitions. Answer any questions about meaning and provide examples of the words in context.

2. Model the pronunciation of each word and have students repeat. Listen for correct syllable stress.

3. Direct students to complete the sentences with the vocabulary words. Have them compare their answers with a partner.

4. Call on volunteers to read the sentences aloud.

> **Vocabulary Answers, pp. 158–159**
> **1.** adopt;   **2.** reunion;   **3.** In all probability;
> **4.** biological;   **5.** alert;   **6.** odds;
> **7.** ache;   **8.** face to face; **9.** miracle;
> **10.** deprived

MULTILEVEL OPTION

Group lower-level students and assist them with the task. Provide example sentences to help them understand the words. For example, *My legs **ached** after I ran ten kilometers. Every year, my family gets together for a **reunion**.*

After higher-level students have completed the activity, have pairs write an additional sentence for each word. Have volunteers write their sentences on the board. Correct the sentences as a class, focusing on the use of the words rather than other grammatical issues.

 For additional practice with the vocabulary, have students visit *Q Online Practice.*

▶ *Listening and Speaking 4, page 159*

PREVIEW LISTENING 2 (5 minutes)

1. Read the introduction aloud.

2. Ask students to consider the question and check their answer. They should then discuss the reasons for their answer with a partner. Tell students they should review their answer after the listening.

> **Preview Listening 2 Answer, p. 159**
> Answers will vary. Possible answers: Yes, they would feel an emotional connection because they shared the beginning of life together. / No, they would not feel a connection because they wouldn't have known that they had a sibling.

Listening 2 Background Note

For various reasons, families might choose to adopt a child instead of have one themselves. The adoption process is not quick or easy. Adoption is a big decision, and everyone wants to ensure the situation ends up as the best decision for all people involved—the biological parents, the adoptive parents, the child, and the governments of both sets of parents.

LISTEN FOR MAIN IDEAS (15 minutes)

CD3, Track 18

1. Have students read the questions.

2. Play the audio as students complete the activity individually.

3. Elicit the answers from volunteers. Ask students what evidence they heard to support the answer.

> **Listen for Main Ideas Answers, pp. 159–160**
> **1.** They first got to know each other through an Internet support group.
> **2.** Renee looked very similar to Annie.
> **3.** They spent the entire reunion together and became best friends.
> **4.** The two girls were considering each other as sisters, and Andrea Ettingoff wanted to make sure they weren't mistaken.
> **5.** The girls are almost certainly fraternal twins.
> **6.** She became very excited and happy.

LISTEN FOR DETAILS (10 minutes)

 CD3, Track 19

1. Direct students to read the questions and answers before they listen again.

2. As you play the audio, have students choose the correct answer.

3. Have students compare answers with a partner.

4. Go over the answers with the class.

   Listen for Details Answers, pp. 160–161
   1. b; **2.** a; **3.** b; **4.** a; **5.** a; **6.** b; **7.** b; **8.** b

   For additional practice with listening comprehension, have students visit *Q Online Practice.*

WHAT DO YOU THINK?

A (15 minutes)

1. Ask students to read the questions and reflect on their answers.

2. Seat students in small groups and assign roles: a group leader to make sure everyone contributes, a note-taker to record the group's ideas, a reporter to share the group's ideas with the class, and a timekeeper to watch the clock.

3. Give students ten minutes to discuss the questions. Call time if conversations are winding down. Allow extra time if necessary.

4. Call on each group's reporter to share ideas with the class.

   Activity A Answers, p. 161
   Answers will vary. Possible answers:
   1. I think it is important for the sisters to get to know each other. I think they should be able to see each other more often. / No, I don't think it is necessary for the girls to develop a relationship. That would be more work for the parents, who live far apart.
   2. I think the girls remembered each other from when they were very young.

B (10 minutes)

1. Have students continue working in their small groups to discuss the questions in Activity B. Tell them to choose a new leader, note-taker, reporter, and timekeeper.

2. Call on the new reporter to share the group's answers to the questions.

Activity B Answers, p. 161
Answers will vary. Possible answers:
1. I don't think all of these discoveries only happened by chance. Preparation, practice, and timing also may have affected what happened.
2. A chance discovery can be negative if that discovery becomes a weapon of war or a chemical that ends up making people ill.

MULTILEVEL OPTION

To complete Activity B in What Do You Think, form mixed-ability groups. Have higher-level students ask lower-level students the questions in B. Have the higher-level students encourage the lower-level ones to give reasons to support their answers.

Learning Outcome

Use the learning outcome to frame the purpose and relevance of Listenings 1 and 2. Ask: *What did you learn that prepares you to recount the events involved in a personal discovery you made accidently and tell how it affected you?* (Students learned about discoveries that happened by chance. They may want to refer to these ideas in their stories about personal discoveries.)

Vocabulary Skill: Collocations with prepositions (15 minutes)

1. Present the information on collocations. Ask volunteers to read the example collocations.

2. Check comprehension: *What is a collocation? What are some examples of collocations with prepositions? How does paying attention to collocations help your fluency?*

Skill Note

The Oxford Collocations Dictionary for students of English contains over 150,000 collocations for nouns, verbs, and adjectives. As students learn new verbs and adjectives, encourage them to look the words up in a collocations dictionary to see which prepositions collocate with the words. A regular dictionary can also be helpful because often the entries themselves or the example sentences in the entries contain collocations.

A (5 minutes)
CD3, Track 20

1. Direct students to preview the statements and guess which prepositions go in the blanks.

2. Play the audio. Have students circle the correct prepositions. Go over the answers with the class.

Activity A Answers, pp. 162–163
1. c; **2.** c; **3.** b; **4.** c

▶ *Listening and Speaking 4, page 163*
Tip for Success (1 minute)

1. Ask a volunteer to read the tip aloud.

2. Ask: *Why is this information an important tip? How can you use this advice to become a better language learner?*

B (5 minutes)

1. Direct students to work individually to complete the task. Then have them check their answers with a partner.

2. Check the answers as a class.

Activity B Answers, p. 163
1. afraid of; **2.** stumbling over; **3.** mixed / with;
4. thank for; **5.** filled / with

 For additional practice with collocations with prepositions, have students visit *Q Online Practice*.

SPEAKING

▶ *Listening and Speaking 4, page 164*
Grammar: Indirect speech (15 minutes)

1. Go over the grammar skill and the examples of direct and indirect speech.

2. Check comprehension by asking questions: *When do we use indirect speech? How do we change indirect speech for the past tense? What rule must we follow when using indirect speech with a wh- question? Can you give an example of indirect speech?*

3. Answer any questions that students still have about indirect speech. Provide additional examples as needed.

A (10 minutes)
🔊 CD3, Track 21

1. Direct students to listen to each sentence and decide whether it is direct or indirect speech.

2. Play the audio. Call on volunteers to share their answers with the class.

Activity A Answers, pp. 164–165
1. b; **2.** a; **3.** a; **4.** b; **5.** b; **6.** b; **7.** b; **8.** a

▶ *Listening and Speaking 4, page 165*
B (15 minutes)

1. Read the directions aloud. Direct students to rewrite the sentences, changing the direct speech to indirect speech.

2. Ask volunteers to write their sentences on the board.

3. Elicit corrections and questions from the class. Then have partners practice saying both versions of each sentence.

Activity B Answers, p. 165
Answers may vary. Possible answers:
1. Martha Teichner said (that) the list of serendipity stories was as long as the history of discovery.
2. The professor said (that) many people use a microwave oven every day.
3. The professor said that he invented something that would revolutionize cooking.
4. The professor said that we see microwave ovens just about everywhere.
5. Andrea said (that) she was shocked.
6. Renee said (that) the hole in her heart was getting smaller.
7. Renee said (that) she was Annie, and Annie said (that) she was Renee.
8. In her message, Eileen said (that) she didn't know if/ whether her baby knew Andrea's baby.

 For additional practice with indirect speech, have students visit *Q Online Practice*.

21ST CENTURY SKILLS

Indirect speech allows someone to report what another person has said. In the workplace, students may be asked to debrief a colleague or supervisor about a meeting or even report this information in meeting notes, which may be distributed to others. Point out to students that it's in situations like these where they may need to use indirect speech.

▶ *Listening and Speaking 4, page 166*
Pronunciation: Linked words with vowels (15 minutes)

🔊 CD3, Track 22

1. Present the pronunciation information and play the audio when noted. Provide additional examples for the linking /y/ and /w/ sounds.

2. Check comprehension by asking questions: *What do we mean when we talk about linking words? What kinds of words are linked together with the /y/ sound? What kinds of words are linked with the /w/ sound?*

Skill Note

When proficient speakers speak, they almost always link words with vowels. If students are able to link the sounds themselves, they will be more likely to hear the links in other people's speech.

A (10 minutes)

CD3, Track 23

1. Play the audio and direct students to repeat after each pair of words.

2. Discuss which pairs are linked with a /y/ sound and which are linked with a /w/ sound.

B (15 minutes)

CD3, Track 24

1. Ask a volunteer to read the directions.

2. Play the audio. Have students mark their answers individually and then compare answers with a partner.

3. Review the answers as a class. Then have partners practice saying the sentences.

Activity B Answers, pp. 166–167
1. Annie*ʸ*also seemed very deprived, because they noticed she*ʸ*ate as if she'd never eat again.
2. After the fact, serendipity*ʸ*always seems so*ʷ*obvious.
3. Because we hardly*ʸ*ever fight, we*ʸ*agree on a lot of things.
4. Eventually somebody*ʸ*else at the company thought maybe*ʸ*it would keep bookmarks from falling out of his hymnal at church.
5. Try*ʸ*and spot the next big thing.
6. So*ʷ*after you*ʷ*opened the file, can you recall how*ʷ*it felt?

 For additional practice with linked words with vowels, have students visit *Q Online Practice*.

Teaching Note

Activity B, item 4, mentions a hymnal. A hymnal is a songbook made up of hymns. A hymn is a song that usually praises a prominent person or a nation.

▶ *Listening and Speaking 4, page 167*

Speaking Skill: Using questions to maintain listener interest (20 minutes)

1. Present the information on using questions to maintain listener interest. Discuss the two types of questions: rhetorical and interactive. Provide additional examples as needed.

2. Check comprehension: *What can a question do at the beginning of a presentation? What is the difference between a rhetorical question and an interactive question? Why do you think questions maintain listener interest?*

A (10 minutes)

CD3, Track 25

1. Direct students to listen to each excerpt and decide whether the question is a rhetorical or interactive question.

2. Play the audio. Ask students to compare their answers with a partner. Then check the answers as a class.

Activity A Answers, p. 167
1. rhetorical; 2. rhetorical;
3. interactive; 4. interactive

▶ *Listening and Speaking 4, page 168*

Tip for Success (1 minute)

1. Read the tip aloud.

2. Explain: *Make sure to give your audience enough time to think about the question and answer. You don't want them to feel rushed.*

B (15 minutes)

CD3, Track 26

1. Play the audio as students read along.

2. Then ask students to answer the questions and compare their answers with a partner. Check the answers as a class.

Activity B Answers, p. 168
1. a; 2. c; 3. b

C (10 minutes)

1. Read the directions for Activity C.

2. Place students in groups to retell the story in Activity B. Remind them to use questions to keep their listeners' interest.

Activity C Answers, p. 168
Answers will vary.

 For additional practice with using questions to maintain listener interest, have students visit *Q Online Practice.*

▶ *Listening and Speaking 4, page 169*

Unit Assignment: Tell a story

Unit Question (5 minutes)

Refer students back to the ideas they discussed at the beginning of the unit about how chance discoveries affect our lives. Cue students if necessary by asking specific questions about the content of the unit: *What is a chance discovery? What chance discoveries made by other people have affected your life? What chance discoveries have you made that have affected your life?* Read the direction lines for the assignment together to ensure understanding.

Learning Outcome

1. Tie the Unit Assignment to the unit learning outcome. Say: *The outcome for this unit is to recount the events involved in a personal discovery you made accidently and tell how it affected you. This Unit Assignment is going to let you show your skill in telling a story as well as using questions to maintain your listeners' interest, using signal words, and linking words with vowels.*

2. Explain that you are going to use a rubric similar to their Self-Assessment checklist on p. 170 to grade their Unit Assignment. Ask students to read the checklist now so they have a specific understanding of how they will be assessed. You can also share a copy of the Unit Assignment Rubric (on p. 88 of this *Teacher's Handbook*) with the students.

Consider the Ideas (15 minutes)

1. Direct students to read the directions for the activity. Ask a volunteer to read the ideas aloud.

2. Have students make their four choices and then discuss their choices with a partner.

3. Ask volunteers to share their choices and reasons with the class.

Prepare to Speak

Gather Ideas

A (10 minutes)

Ask students to read the directions and work individually to write notes from their discussions.

Organize Ideas

B (15 minutes)

1. Read the directions aloud.

2. Ask students to expand upon their ideas from Activity A by thinking about their answer to item 1 and completing the chart in item 2.

3. Circulate around the room and offer support.

Critical Thinking Tip (3 minutes)

1. Read the Critical Thinking Tip aloud.

2. Briefly discuss how combining ideas and experience can be helpful in understanding a situation.

Critical Q: Expansion Activity

Combine Ideas

Present students with two scenarios that involve hands-on creation of something (e.g., making a shelter in the forest or making a receptacle to carry water). Tell students they only have certain tools to solve their problem: strong tape (duct tape), paperclips, a 1 x 1 meter sheet of plastic, and a one-meter plastic tube.

Have students work in groups of three or four. For each scenario, have students look at each "tool" in a new way to discover a unique solution to the problem. Encourage students to combine creativity with personal experience to design things.

▶ *Listening and Speaking 4, page 170*

Speak

C (30–45 minutes)

1. Go over the directions. Call on students to present their story to the class.

2. Use the Unit Assignment Rubric on p. 88 of this *Teacher's Handbook* to score each student's presentation.

3. Alternatively, divide the class into large groups and have students tell their stories to their groups. Have listeners complete the Unit Assignment Rubric, making sure there are enough copies for all students.

Alternative Unit Assignments

Assign or have students choose one of these assignments to do instead of, or in addition to, the Unit Assignment.

1. Interview friends or family members and ask them to share stories about personal discoveries or coincidences in their lives. Take notes on their experiences and then report your findings to your classmates.

2. Do online research to find a "strange but true" news story to share with your classmates. Take notes on the events in the story so that you can explain it in your own words. When searching for these stories online, use keywords such as *wacky news* and *strange but true news*.

 For an additional Unit Assignment, have students visit *Q Online Practice*.

Check and Reflect

Check

A (10 minutes)

1. Direct students to read and complete the Self-Assessment checklist.

2. Ask for a show of hands for how many students gave all or mostly *yes* answers. Congratulate them on their success.

3. Remind students that they can always refer to the checklist before they begin the Unit Assignment so they can focus on the skills they need to complete the assignment successfully. Have students discuss with a partner what they can improve for next time.

Reflect

B (10 minutes)

Ask students to consider the questions in pairs. When the conversations have died down, have students share something new they have learned. Ask: *How did your ideas about how chance discoveries affect our lives change as we worked through the unit?*

▶ *Listening and Speaking 4, page 171*

Track Your Success (5 minutes)

1. Have students circle the words they have learned in this unit. Suggest that students go back through the unit to review any words they have forgotten.

2. Have students check the skills they have mastered. If students need more practice to feel confident about their proficiency in a skill, point out the page numbers and encourage them to review.

3. Read the learning outcome aloud *(Recount the events involved in a personal discovery you made accidently and tell how it affected you)*. Ask students if they feel that they have met the outcome.

Unit Assignment Rubric

Student name: _____

Date: _____

Unit Assignment: *Tell a story.*

20 points = Story element was completely successful (at least 90% of the time).
15 points = Story element was mostly successful (at least 70% of the time).
10 points = Story element was partially successful (at least 50% of the time).
 0 points = Story element was not successful.

Tell a Story	20 points	15 points	10 points	0 points
Student clearly explained events involved in their discovery and provided details.				
Student used signal words correctly.				
Student linked words with vowels correctly.				
Student used questions to maintain listener interest.				
Student used vocabulary from the unit.				

Total points: _____

Comments:

9

Unit QUESTION
How can we maintain a balance with nature?

Humans and Nature

LISTENING • listening carefully to an introduction
VOCABULARY • word forms
GRAMMAR • relative clauses
PRONUNCIATION • reduced forms
SPEAKING • using persuasive language

LEARNING OUTCOME

Role-play a meeting in which you present and defend an opinion in order to persuade others.

▶ *Listening and Speaking 4, page 173*
Preview the Unit

Learning Outcome

1. Ask a volunteer to read the unit skills and then the unit learning outcome.

2. Explain: *This is what you are expected to be able to do by the unit's end. The learning outcome explains how you are going to be evaluated. With this outcome in mind, you should focus on learning these skills (Listening, Vocabulary, Grammar, Pronunciation, Speaking) that will support your goal of role-playing a meeting in which you present and defend an opinion in order to persuade others. This can also help you act as mentors in the classroom to help the other students meet this outcome.*

A (15 minutes)

1. Write the word *Nature* on the board and have students come up to the board and write words that they think relate to nature (e.g., *oceans, air, forest*).

2. Put students in pairs or small groups to discuss the first two questions.

3. Call on volunteers to share their ideas with the class. Ask questions: *Do you think people need to live in balance with nature? Why or why not? How do you find a balance with nature in your life?*

4. Direct students' attention to the photo. Have a volunteer describe the photo. Read the third question aloud. Elicit students' answers.

> **Activity A Answers, p. 173**
> Answers will vary. Possible answers:
> **1.** My neighbors and I go down to the river and pick up trash that people leave there. A coworker donates money to a local organization that does a lot of work to protect the environment.

> **2.** I think we should stop cutting down trees in the quantity that we do. We need to protect the forests where animals live.
> **3.** People like to watch animals play because it helps them learn about animals' behavior.

B (15 minutes)

1. Introduce the Unit Question, *How can we maintain a balance with nature?* Ask related information questions or questions about personal experience to help students prepare for answering the more abstract Unit Question. Ask: *Does nature need to be protected? Why or why not? Do you think that people do enough to protect nature? If yes, why? If not, what else can they do?*

2. Label four pieces of poster paper with four interesting answers to the Unit Question (e.g., *leave habitats wild, plant more trees in the forest, use fewer natural resources,* and *spend more time appreciating nature*). Place each answer in a different corner of the room.

3. Ask students to consider the Unit Question and then stand next to the poster that best represents their answer to the question. If all students stand by only one or two options, have some students stand by the answer that represents their second or third choices.

4. Direct the groups in each corner to talk amongst themselves about the reasons for their answer. Tell them to choose a note-taker to record their ideas on the poster paper.

5. Call on a volunteer from each corner to share the group's ideas with the class. Keep the posters for students to refer back to at the end of the unit.

The Q Classroom

 CD4, Track 2

1. Play The Q Classroom. Use the example from the audio to help students continue the conversation. Ask: *How did the students answer the question? Do you agree or disagree with their ideas? Why?*

2. Say: *Marcus says that to protect nature, people need to buy fewer things. Do you agree with him? Will that help? Why or why not?*

▶ *Listening and Speaking 4, page 174*

C (10 minutes)

1. Ask a volunteer to read the directions aloud.

2. Have students work individually to rank the issues. Then have students compare their rankings with a partner.

3. Discuss the students' rankings as a class.

D (10 minutes)

1. Direct students to preview the list and check their answers.

2. Pair students and have them compare answers.

3. Choose a few volunteers to share their answers with the class.

LISTENING

▶ *Listening and Speaking 4, page 175*

LISTENING 1: Polar Bears at Risk

VOCABULARY (20 minutes)

1. Direct students to read each sentence and try to guess what the word in bold means. Remind them to use context clues for help. Then have them write the word next to the correct definition.

2. Have students compare answers with a partner.

3. Elicit the answers from volunteers. Model the pronunciation of each word and have students repeat. Check for correct syllable stress.

MULTILEVEL OPTION

Group lower-level students and assist them with the task. Provide alternate example sentences to help them understand the words. For example, *Global warming is **devastating** the polar bears' habitat, so they have very few places to live. The antique vase was very old and **fragile**.*

Have higher-level students write an additional sentence for each word. Ask volunteers to write their sentences on the board. Correct the sentences as a class.

Vocabulary Answers, pp. 175–176

a. meager;	**b.** refuge;	**c.** decrease;
d. decade;	**e.** fragile;	**f.** crisis;
g. potentially;	**h.** adapt;	**i.** grip;
j. retreat;	**k.** alarming;	**l.** devastating

 For additional practice with the vocabulary, have students visit *Q Online Practice*.

▶ *Listening and Speaking 4, page 176*

PREVIEW LISTENING 1 (5 minutes)

1. Before students begin this activity, ask: *What would you do if someone ruined your house so you couldn't live there anymore?*

2. Read the introduction aloud. Place students into mixed-ability pairs and have them discuss the question. Tell students they should review their answers after the listening.

Preview Listening 1 Answer, p. 176
Answers will vary. Possible answer: The polar bears would die.

Listening 1 Background Note

The Wrangel Island Reserve is a UNESCO World Heritage Site. (UNESCO stands for United Nations Educational, Scientific and Cultural Organization.) Besides being a weather station and a fishing stop in the Arctic, Wrangel Island is interesting for other reasons. The yearly average temperature on the island is a high of -8°C and a low of -14°C. The island is believed to be the last place that wooly mammoths lived, having died out 4,000 years ago.

LISTEN FOR MAIN IDEAS (15 minutes)

 CD4, Track 3

1. Preview the questions with the students.

2. Play the audio and have students complete the activity individually.

3. Ask volunteers to share their answers with the class.

> **Listen for Main Ideas Answers, pp. 176–177**
> 1. To do research on the polar bears
> 2. The polar bear population is smaller; Polar bears are smaller in size; Winter ends earlier. (Students should list two.)
> 3. The ice is melting earlier; The hunting season is shorter.
> 4. They stand on the ice to hunt.
> 5. Hunting is more difficult; The hunting season is shorter; They have to go farther to find food.
> 6. Create land refuges

Tip for Success (1 minute)

1. Read the tip aloud.
2. Encourage students to keep a vocabulary journal where they write down new words, the sentences they found them in, and the definitions of those words.

 Listening and Speaking 4, page 177
LISTEN FOR DETAILS (10 minutes)

 CD4, Track 4

1. Direct students to read the questions and answer choices before they listen again.
2. As you play the audio, have students circle the best answer.
3. Have students compare answers with a partner. Replay the audio if necessary.
5. Go over the answers with the class.

> **Listen for Details Answers, p. 177**
> **1.** c; **2.** c; **3.** c; **4.** a; **5.** b

 For additional practice with listening comprehension, have students visit *Q Online Practice.*

 Listening and Speaking 4, page 178
WHAT DO YOU THINK? (15 minutes)

1. Ask students to read the questions and reflect on their answers.
2. Seat students in small groups and assign roles: a group leader to make sure everyone contributes, a note-taker to record the group's ideas, a reporter to share the group's ideas with the class, and a timekeeper to watch the clock.

3. Give students ten minutes to discuss the questions. Call time if conversations are winding down. Allow them an extra minute or two if necessary
4. Call on each group's reporter to share ideas with the class.

MULTILEVEL OPTION

Place students into mixed-ability pairs. Higher-level students can support lower-level students during the discussion.

What Do You Think? Answers, p. 178
Answers will vary. Possible answers:
1. We might help polar bears survive climate change if we reverse the impact we've had on the world's temperatures. We need to use fewer resources, drive less, and use cleaner energy.
2. Governments do this because they want to protect animals that symbolize their countries.

Learning Outcome

Use the learning outcome to frame the purpose and relevance of Listening 1. Ask: *What did you learn from Listening 1 that prepares you to role-play a meeting in which you present and defend an opinion in order to persuade others?* (Students learned how climate change is affecting the polar bear's habitat. They may want to use this information in their role-plays.)

Listening Skill: Listening carefully to an introduction (15 minutes)

1. Present the information on listening to an introduction.
2. Check comprehension by asking questions: *Why should you listen carefully to an introduction? What are some examples of organizational phrases? What kinds of things should you listen for in an introduction?*

 Listening and Speaking 4, page 179
A (15 minutes)
 CD4, Track 5

1. Read the directions aloud. Ask students to scan the speech silently before you play the audio.
2. Play the audio as students read along and then mark the text.
3. Ask students to compare their marks with a partner. Then go over the marks as a class. You may want to project the paragraph to highlight the marks.

Activity A Answers, p. 179

Hello! Um, today, I want to continue our discussion about the <u>impact</u> of <u>human</u> behavior, specifically <u>pollution</u>, on the <u>environment</u>. I want to draw your attention to the <u>effect</u> <u>humans</u> are having on one of the smaller animals with which we share the planet: <u>honey bees</u>. You might be thinking, "<u>Why should we care about honey bees?</u>" Well, <u>in the first part of this lecture,</u> I'll explain the important role <u>honey bees</u> play in our daily lives. You might be surprised to find out just how vital their health is to you! <u>In the second half of the lecture,</u> I'll review some recent research on how <u>pollution</u> in the <u>environment</u> is causing flowers to lose their <u>smell</u>. I'll also talk about how the <u>bees</u> are confused by this lack of <u>smell</u>. <u>Finally, we'll finish up</u> today with my predictions for the future for <u>bees</u> and, consequently, for <u>humans</u>. OK, let's get started ...

B (10 minutes)

1. Have students refer to the lecture introduction as they answer the questions.

2. When students finish, have them check answers in pairs. Confirm the answers as a class.

Activity B Answers, p. 179

Answers will vary. Possible answers:
1. the impact of human behavior on the environment
2. how humans are affecting honey bees
3. why they are losing their smell
4. the importance of honey bees; pollution causing flowers to lose their smell, the effect on bees, and predictions for future

 For additional practice with listening carefully to an introduction, have students visit *Q Online Practice.*

▶ *Listening and Speaking 4, page 180*

LISTENING 2: The Effects of Oil Spills

VOCABULARY (15 minutes)

1. Direct students to read each sentence and try to guess what the word in bold means. Remind them to use context clues for help. Then students should circle the correct definition for the bold word.

2. Have students compare answers with a partner. Then call on volunteers for the answers.

3. Model the pronunciation of each vocabulary word and have students repeat. Listen for correct syllable stress.

Vocabulary Answers, pp. 180–181
1. c; **2.** a; **3.** b; **4.** b; **5.** a; **6.** a;
7. b; **8.** b; **9.** c; **10.** b; **11.** c; **12.** a

 For additional practice with the vocabulary, have students visit *Q Online Practice.*

▶ *Listening and Speaking 4, page 181*

PREVIEW LISTENING 2 (5 minutes)

1. Direct students' attention to the photo and ask: *What do you think is in these barrels?*

2. Read the introduction aloud. Have students discuss their answers to the questions in pairs. Tell students they should review their answers after the listening.

Preview Listening 2 Answer, p. 182

Answers will vary. Possible answers: An oil spill damages the environment, so animals will have difficulty finding food. Also, they will become covered in oil, which makes it hard to swim. An oil spill might also cause fisherman to lose their jobs because they can't fish in the affected waters.

Listening 2 Background Note

The Exxon Valdez oil spill is still having an impact on the environment—over 20 years after it happened. In a similar fashion, the BP oil spill (sometimes also called the Deepwater Horizon oil spill) in the Gulf of Mexico—larger in volume than the Exxon Valdez oil spill—has caused major environmental problems in that sensitive region. Scientists will need to study the effects of the spill on the plant and animal species in the Gulf for many years to come.

▶ *Listening and Speaking 4, page 182*

LISTEN FOR MAIN IDEAS (10 minutes)

 CD4, Track 6

1. Have students preview the statements in pairs.

2. Play the audio and have students complete the activity individually.

3. Check the answers as a class.

> **Listen for Main Ideas Answers, p. 182**
> Checked: The Exxon Valdez spill was one of the worst environmental disasters in U.S. history; Many of the problems were caused by the location of Prince William Sound; The spill still affects the area many years later; Many animals suffered and died because of the oil spill; People are working on new ways to deal with oil spills.

LISTEN FOR DETAILS (10 minutes)

CD4, Track 7

A (10 minutes)

1. Direct students to read the statements before they listen again.

2. As you play the audio, have students mark the statements *T* or *F*.

3. Have students compare answers with a partner. Replay the audio so partners can check their answers.

4. Go over the answers with the class. Elicit corrections for the false statements.

> **Activity A Answers, pp. 182–183**
> **1.** F; **2.** F; **3.** T; **4.** F; **5.** T;
> **6.** F; **7.** T; **8.** F; **9.** T; **10.** T

▶ *Listening and Speaking 4, page 183*

B (10 minutes)

1. Direct students to answer the questions and then compare answers with a partner.

2. Go over the answers with the class.

> **Activity B Answers, p. 183**
> Answers will vary. Possible answers:
> **1.** Hot water killed bacteria that help break down oil.
> **2.** It will last indefinitely.
> **3.** It has cost about $2.1 billion so far.

 For additional practice with listening comprehension, have students visit *Q Online Practice*.

WHAT DO YOU THINK?

A (15 minutes)

1. Ask students to read the questions and reflect on their answers.

2. Seat students in small groups and assign roles: a group leader to make sure everyone contributes, a note-taker to record the group's ideas, a reporter to share the group's ideas with the class, and a timekeeper to watch the clock.

3. Give students ten minutes to discuss the questions. Call time if conversations are winding down. Allow extra time if necessary.

4. Call on each group's reporter to share ideas with the class.

> **Activity A Answers, p. 183**
> Answers will vary. Possible answers:
> **1.** Environmental problems can happen where I live because people are always interacting with nature.
> **2.** I could volunteer to help clean up, or I could help educate people about why this disaster happened and how to avoid it in the future.
> **3.** I don't know if my community has a plan. I could ask the local government office to find out.

B (10 minutes)

1. Have students continue working in their small groups to discuss the questions in Activity B. Tell them to choose a new leader, note-taker, reporter, and timekeeper.

2. Call on the new reporter to share the group's answers to the questions.

> **Activity B Answers, p. 183**
> Answers will vary. Possible answers:
> **1.** I think the shrinking polar bear habitat is more serious because the polar bear may become extinct. / I think the damage done by the oil spill is more serious because it affects both animals and humans.
> **2.** Scientists will need to continue to study the long-term effects of both problems and propose solutions. In both situations, scientists are working to help wildlife recover. However, the solutions to both problems will be different because their locations are different—the Arctic and Prince William Sound.

Critical Thinking Tip (1 minute)

1. Ask a volunteer to read the Critical Thinking Tip.

2. Explain to students that using a chart or Venn diagram can help them organize their ideas when they compare and contrast.

Compare and Contrast

Pair students up and have them use the Internet to research the Exxon-Valdez oil spill of 1989 and the BP oil spill of 2010. Direct the students' research so that they find information that compares and contrasts the two incidents.

Provide a graphic organizer, such as a chart or Venn diagram for students to record the information they find. Have students present their findings to the class.

Learning Outcome

Use the learning outcome to frame the purpose and relevance of Listenings 1 and 2 and the Critical Q activity. Ask: *What did you learn that prepares you to role-play a meeting in which you present and defend an opinion in order to persuade others?* (Students learned about serious environmental problems in two different places on Earth. They may want to refer to these ideas in their role-plays.)

▶ *Listening and Speaking 4, page 184*

Vocabulary Skill: Word forms (15 minutes)

1. Probe for previous knowledge by asking: *What is a suffix? Can you give some examples?*

2. Present the information on suffixes. Ask volunteers to read the suffixes and example words.

3. Check comprehension: *What is a suffix? What does -ify make—a noun or a verb? What does –able make—an adverb or an adjective? What are some example suffixes for nouns?*

Skill Note

Being able to recognize suffixes will help students figure out the meanings of words. As students read texts in class, encourage them to identify any words that contain suffixes, determine the part of speech, and guess what the words mean. You may also want to encourage students to organize a part of their notebooks to list words with suffixes that they encounter in class.

EXPANSION ACTIVITY: Using Suffixes (25 minutes)

1. To help reinforce suffix use, quiz students on the vocabulary from this unit. Give them four minutes to write as many of the unit's vocabulary words as they can think of.

2. Place students into pairs and ask them to combine their lists. Have students use the words on their list to write as many word forms as they can (e.g., *fragile, fragility; devastating, devastation*). Encourage students to use their dictionaries for help.

3. Check the word forms as a class and have students try to use the new words in sentences.

A (10 minutes)

1. Go over the directions. Ask students to underline the suffix in each word (e.g., *diversify*).

2. Direct students to complete the activity individually.

3. Go over the answers with the class.

> **Activity A Answers, p. 184**
> **1.** noun;   **2.** adjective;   **3.** verb;   **4.** adjective;
> **5.** noun;   **6.** noun;   **7.** verb;   **8.** adjective;
> **9.** adverb;   **10.** verb

▶ *Listening and Speaking 4, page 185*

B (10 minutes)

1. Read the directions aloud.

2. Ask students to complete the activity individually. They may want to use a dictionary for help. Then have students check their answers with a partner.

3. Check the answers as a class.

> **Activity B Answers, p. 185**
> **1.** biologist;   **2.** national;   **3.** dramatic;
> **4.** definitely;   **5.** commercial;   **6.** categorize;
> **7.** devastating;   **8.** commercially;   **9.** apologize;
> **10.** division

SPEAKING

▶ *Listening and Speaking 4, page 186*

Grammar: Relative clauses (20 minutes)

1. Ask volunteers to read the information aloud. Stop at logical points and provide additional explanation or examples as needed.

2. Check comprehension by asking: *What kinds of relative clauses are there? What's the difference between restrictive and non-restrictive relative clauses? What are some relative pronouns used with restrictive clauses? With non-restrictive?* Ask volunteers to provide example sentences using relative clauses.

Listening and Speaking 4, page 187

A (10 minutes)

1. Have a student read the directions for the activity. Go over item 1 as a class.

2. Have students complete the task individually and then compare answers with a partner.

3. Go over the answers with the class. Discuss why the clauses are restrictive or nonrestrictive.

> **Activity A Answers, p. 187**
> R **1.** which scientists believe is caused by climate change
> R **2.** that it will need to stay alive
> NR **3.** which is in the northeast part of Prince William Sound
> NR **4.** which is toxic to birds
> NR **5.** which protect birds and animals from the cold
> R **6.** that ate oil-covered seals
> R **7.** that live in Prince William Sound
> R **8.** that can skim the oil off the surface of the water
> NR **9.** which basically eat the oil
> R **10.** that promotes the growth of the bacteria

B (10 minutes)

1. Read the directions and relative clauses with the class.

2. Direct students to complete the activity and then compare answers in pairs. Review the answers as a class.

> **Activity B Answers, pp. 187–188**
> **1.** who work on Wrangel Island
> **2.** which has been going on for ten years
> **3.** which is part Russia
> **4.** that are adapted to the cold
> **5.** that the oil spill affected
> **6.** which are creatures of the ice
> **7.** which were closed right after the oil spill
> **8.** which was a commercial oil tanker
> **9.** which retreats in the summer
> **10.** which is around 25,000 worldwide

 For additional practice with relative clauses, have students visit *Q Online Practice*.

 Listening and Speaking 4, page 188

Pronunciation: Reduced forms (15 minutes)

 CD4, Track 8

1. Present the information on reduced forms, playing the audio when noted. Elicit and answer questions students have.

2. Check comprehension by asking questions: *When do we shorten words? What words are often reduced?*

Listening and Speaking 4, page 189

A (15 minutes)

CD4, Track 9

1. Direct students to read through the conversation with a partner and think about what sounds might be reduced.

2. Play the audio and have students underline the reduced sounds.

3. Put students in pairs to compare their marks. Play the audio again if necessary.

4. Call on volunteers to share their marks with the class. You may want to project the conversation to mark the reduced sounds. Then have pairs practice the conversation.

> **Activity A Answers, p. 189**
> **Sasha:** People are; that are
> **Brian:** For instance
> **Sasha:** that are
> **Sasha:** about them; change is;
> **Brian:** Akbar is; when he; using them

B (10 minutes)

1. Ask a volunteer to read the directions.

2. Have students complete the activity in pairs. Remind students to listen for reduced sounds when their partner talks.

3. Circulate around the room to offer feedback.

For additional practice with reduced forms, have students visit *Q Online Practice*.

Listening and Speaking 4, page 190

Speaking Skill: Using persuasive language (10 minutes)

1. Ask: *How do you try to persuade someone when you are speaking?*

2. Present the information on persuasive language. Call on volunteers to read the strategies.

3. Check comprehension: *What are five ways people can try to persuade others in a conversation? What specific phrases can people use?*

4. You may want to create a poster that lists the five strategies. Students could refer to the poster during their Unit Assignment.

A (25 minutes)

CD4, Track 10

1. Have a volunteer read the directions aloud.

2. Play the audio and have students fill in the blanks.

3. Put students into pairs to compare answers.

4. Check answers as a class.

5. Direct students to answer the final four questions in Activity A. Discuss the answers as a class.

> **Activity A Answers, pp. 190–191**
> don't really think; I mean; I heard; many people believe; think about
> **1.** mentioning expert sources
> **2.** that climate change is new
> **3.** appealing to emotions
> **4.** Answers will vary.

Tip for Success (1 minute)

1. Read the tip aloud.

2. Relate this tip to classroom culture where students are encouraged to raise their hands and ask questions without the teacher prompting them.

▶ *Listening and Speaking 4, page 192*

B (20 minutes)

1. Place students into groups of three or four and have them read the directions to the activity.

2. Have students complete the activity in their groups. Circulate around the room to answer questions as needed.

3. Pair groups up so that they can present their radio ads to each other.

 For additional practice with using persuasive language, have students visit *Q Online Practice*.

21ST CENTURY SKILLS

Businesses need to make the case for why their product or service is better than anyone else's. Students who work in sales or retail, for example, may need to use persuasive language when speaking to a customer. Therefore, practice with persuasive language is a good introduction to an important skill that extends beyond the classroom. To practice this skill more, have students select a product they like to use and persuade other students to buy and use the product as well. Have students report their success (or lack of success) in persuading their classmates.

▶ *Listening and Speaking 4, page 193*

Q Unit Assignment: Persuade a Group

Unit Question (5 minutes)

Refer students back to the ideas they discussed at the beginning of the unit about how to maintain a balance with nature. Pull out the lists from Activity B at the beginning of the unit and have students reflect on their answers. Cue students if necessary by asking specific questions about the content of the unit: *How are polar bears being affected by humans? How are humans affecting nature? What can be done to balance human needs with protecting nature?* Read the direction lines for the assignment together to ensure understanding.

Learning Outcome

1. Tie the Unit Assignment to the unit learning outcome. Say: *The outcome for this unit is to role-play a meeting in which you present and defend an opinion in order to persuade others. This Unit Assignment is going to let you show your skill in persuading a group as well as using relative clauses, persuasive language, and reduced forms.*

2. Explain that you are going to use a rubric similar to their Self-Assessment checklist on p. 196 to grade their Unit Assignment. Share with students a copy of the rubric on p. 98 of this *Teacher's Handbook* so they have a specific understanding of how they will be assessed.

Consider the Ideas (15 minutes)

CD4, Track 11

1. Read the directions and preview the questions as a class.

2. Play the audio. Ask students to write a few notes as an answer for each question. Direct students to discuss their answers with a partner.

3. Elicit the answers from volunteers.

> **Consider the Ideas Answers, p. 193**
> **1.** They need to use the area as a source of income.
> **2.** They don't want to repeat the problems from the past.
> **3.** The mayor hopes that people will share ideas about the best way to develop the land.

Prepare and Speak

Gather Ideas

A (15 minutes)

1. Place students in groups of five.

2. Ask students to read the directions and choose a role or if necessary, assign the roles.

3. Direct students to read the text for their respective role, circle the plan that role has for Clear Lake, and underline statements that support their arguments.

▶ *Listening and Speaking 4, page 195*

Organize Ideas

B (15 minutes)

1. Form groups of students who have the same role.

2. Ask students to work through the questions together to strengthen their arguments. Remind students to try to use vocabulary and grammar from the unit in their responses.

Speak

C (30 minutes)

1. Ask students to return to their original groups and begin the town hall role-play. Make sure students understand the directions before beginning. Call time after 15–20 minutes. Have the "mayor" give clear reasons why he or she was persuaded.

2. Use the Unit Assignment Rubric on p. 98 of this *Teacher's Handbook* to score each student's part of the role-play.

3. Alternatively, have each group present their role-play to the class. Have listeners complete the Unit Assignment Rubric, scoring students individually.

Alternative Unit Assignments

Assign or have students choose one of these assignments to do instead of, or in addition to, the Unit Assignment.

1. Do online research on an endangered species. Report to the class the steps being taken to protect this animal.

2. Work in small groups. Consider ways you could improve the environment of the community where you live. Come up with a list of environmentally friendly ideas to improve public transportation, shopping, housing, schooling, and leisure activities.

 For an additional Unit Assignment, have students visit *Q Online Practice*.

▶ *Listening and Speaking 4, page 197*

Check and Reflect

Check

A (10 minutes)

1. Direct students to read and complete the Self-Assessment checklist.

2. Ask for a show of hands for how many students gave all or mostly *yes* answers. Congratulate them on their success.

3. Remind students that they can always refer to the checklist before they begin the Unit Assignment so they can focus on the skills they need to complete the assignment successfully. Have students discuss with a partner what they can improve for next time.

Reflect

B (10 minutes)

Ask students to consider the questions in pairs. When the conversations have died down, have students share someting new they learned. Ask: *How did your ideas about humans and nature change as we worked through the unit?*

▶ *Listening and Speaking 4, page 197*

Track Your Success (10 minutes)

1. Have students circle the words they have learned in this unit. Suggest that students go back through the unit to review any words they have forgotten.

2. Have students check the skills they have mastered. If students need more practice to feel confident about their proficiency in a skill, point out the page numbers and encourage them to review.

3. Read the learning outcome aloud *(Role-play a meeting in which you present and defend an opinion in order to persuade others)*. Ask students if they feel that they have met the outcome.

Unit Assignment Rubric

Student name: _____

Date: _____

Unit Assignment: *Persuade a group.*

20 points = Presentation element was completely successful (at least 90% of the time).
15 points = Presentation element was mostly successful (at least 70% of the time).
10 points = Presentation element was partially successful (at least 50% of the time).
 0 points = Presentation element was not successful.

Persuade a Group	20 points	15 points	10 points	0 points
Student spoke persuasively to convince the mayor of his or her opinion. (Or, the student who was the mayor made a thoughtful decision based on others' arguments.)				
Student used vocabulary from the unit.				
Student used relative clauses correctly.				
Student used persuasive language.				
Student used reduced forms of words correctly.				

Total points: _____

Comments:

Unit QUESTION

Is athletic competition good for children?

Child's Play

LISTENING • listening for causes and effects
VOCABULARY • idioms
GRAMMAR • uses of real conditionals
PRONUNCIATION • thought groups
SPEAKING • adding to another speaker's comments

LEARNING OUTCOME

Participate in a group discussion about how to encourage children to exhibit good sportsmanship.

▶ *Listening and Speaking 4, page 199*

Preview the Unit

Learning Outcome

1. Ask a volunteer to read the unit skills and then the unit learning outcome.

2. Explain: *This is what you are expected to be able to do by the unit's end. The learning outcome explains how you are going to be evaluated. With this outcome in mind, you should focus on learning these skills (Listening, Vocabulary, Grammar, Pronunciation, Speaking) that will support your goal of participating in a group discussion about how to encourage children to exhibit good sportsmanship. This can also help you act as mentors in the classroom to help the other students meet this outcome.*

A (15 minutes)

1. Elicit students' ideas about competition. Ask: *What is good about competition? What can be negative about competition?*

2. Put students in pairs or small groups to discuss the first two questions.

3. Call on volunteers to share their ideas with the class. Ask questions: *Why do you think competitive sports have developed in many societies? Do societies need sports? Why or why not?*

4. Focus students' attention on the photo. Have a volunteer describe the photo to the class. Read the third question aloud. Elicit students' answers.

Activity A Answers, p. 199
Answers will vary. Possible answers:
1. I played football when I was a kid, and I really liked it because it was fun to play a game with my friends.

2. I think that parents need to be supportive and realistic—not everyone can become a professional athlete, but everyone should be allowed to follow his or her dreams. Children should work hard toward their goals but still make time for play.
3. Children can learn that no matter if you win or lose, it's important to be respectful of the other team.

B (15 minutes)

1. Introduce the Unit Question, *Is athletic competition good for children?* Ask related information questions or questions about personal experience to help students prepare for answering the more abstract Unit Question. Ask: *What kinds of competitions have you been involved in? How did you feel about competing? Was it a positive or negative experience? Why or why not?*

2. Read the Unit Question aloud. Give students a minute to silently consider their answers to the question. Then ask students who would answer *yes* to stand on one side of the room and students who would answer *no* to stand on the other side of the room.

3. Direct students to tell the person next to them their reasons for choosing the answer they did.

4. Call on volunteers from each side to share their opinions with the class.

5. After students have shared their opinions, provide an opportunity for anyone who would like to change sides to do so.

6. Ask students to sit down, copy the Unit Question, and make a note of their answers. The class will refer to these notes at the end of the unit.

Answers will vary. Possible answers: Competition is not good for children because they can feel bad if they lose. / Competition is good for children because they learn to work hard for a goal. / Competition is good for children because they learn how to follow rules and be the best they can be.

The Q Classroom

CD4, Track 12

1. Play The Q Classroom. Use the example from the audio to help students continue the conversation. Ask: *How did the students answer the question? What do you think about their ideas?*

2. Say: *In the audio, Sophy notes that athletic competition teaches children "self-discipline." What does she mean? What is self-discipline, and how does athletic competition teach this skill?*

▶ *Listening and Speaking 4, page 200*

C (15 minutes)

1. Have a volunteer read the directions aloud. Ask students to make their choices individually and then discuss them with a partner.

2. Then divide the room into three sections: *benefit*, *disadvantage*, or *neither* (place signs around the room for each section). Read each outcome and have students stand in the section of the classroom that corresponds to their choice.

3. Have students in each section discuss why they chose their answer. Call on volunteers to share their reasons with the class.

D (15 minutes)

1. Read the directions aloud.

2. Have students work individually to choose their answer. Then put students in pairs and have them share their answers.

3. Walk around the room and listen to their answers. Select a few model answers and ask those students to share their thoughts with the entire class.

▶ *Listening and Speaking 4, page 201*

LISTENING

LISTENING 1:
Training Chinese Athletes

VOCABULARY (15 minutes)

1. Direct students to read each sentence and try to guess what the word in bold means. Remind them to use context clues for help. Then have students write the word next to the correct definition.

2. Elicit the answers from volunteers. Discuss the context clues in the sentences.

3. Model the pronunciation of each word and have students repeat. Listen for correct syllable stress.

Vocabulary Answers, pp. 201–202

a. era;	**b.** integral;	**c.** apex;
d. brutal;	**e.** collapse;	**f.** dominate;
g. intensity;	**h.** beneficiary;	**i.** funding;
j. invest;	**k.** conclude;	**l.** modest

MULTILEVEL OPTION

Place students in mixed-ability pairs. The higher-level students can assist lower-level students in filling in the blanks and explain their understanding of the meaning of the words. Direct students to alternate reading the sentences aloud. Encourage them to help each other with pronunciation.

 For additional practice with the vocabulary, have students visit *Q Online Practice*.

▶ *Listening and Speaking 4, page 202*

PREVIEW LISTENING 1 (5 minutes)

1. Direct students to read the introduction and complete the activity individually. Then have them share their answers with a partner.

2. Tell students they should review their answers after listening.

Preview Listening 1 Answer, p. 202
Answers will vary.

Listening 1 Background Note

The Olympics have long been an event where nations compete for something besides medals; they compete for honor and prestige. Originally held in Olympia,

Greece, more than 2,500 years ago, the summer and winter Olympics are hosted during even-numbered years in various countries.

LISTEN FOR MAIN IDEAS (15 minutes)

)) CD4, Track 13

1. Have students preview the statements and answer choices.

2. Play the audio and have students complete the activity individually.

3. Ask volunteers to share their answers with the class. Ask these students to provide details from the listening to support their answers.

> Listen for Main Ideas Answers, pp. 202–203
> **1.** b; **2.** c; **3.** a; **4.** a; **5.** c

▶ *Listening and Speaking 4, page 203*

LISTEN FOR DETAILS (15 minutes)

)) CD4, Track 14

1. Direct students to read the statements before they listen again. As you play the audio, have students listen and write *T* or *F.*

2. Have students compare answers with a partner.

3. Ask a volunteer to read the statements. Have students raise their left hands for *false* and their right hands for *true.* Elicit corrections for the false statements.

> Listen for Details Answers, p. 203
> **1.** F; **2.** T; **3.** T; **4.** T; **5.** F; **6.** F

 For additional practice with listening comprehension, have students visit *Q Online Practice.*

▶ *Listening and Speaking 4, page 204*

WHAT DO YOU THINK? (15 minutes)

1. Ask students to read the questions and reflect on their answers.

2. Seat students in small groups and assign roles: a group leader to make sure everyone contributes, a note-taker to record the group's ideas, a reporter to share the group's ideas with the class, and a timekeeper to watch the clock.

3. Give students ten minutes to discuss the questions. Call time if conversations are winding down. Allow extra time if necessary.

4. Call on each group's reporter to share ideas with the class.

> **What Do You Think? Answers, p. 204**
> **1.** Parents make these kinds of sacrifices because they want what is best for their children and they want to see their children succeed.
> **2.** I think it's better to raise your children to succeed and train them to share because you can't always train your children to be successful. You can teach your children what success is about and model success for them, but they have to succeed themselves.

Critical Thinking Tip (3 minutes)

1. Read the Critical Thinking Tip aloud.

2. Have students briefly discuss when they have used this skill previously in the classroom.

Critical Q: Expansion Activity

Appraise

Place students into groups of three. Have them make a list of situations where they've had to appraise different ideas and make judgments. Once each group has a list, have students discuss how they came to make the judgments that they did.

As a class, ask students: *What factors caused you to come to the judgment you did in the situations you listed? What is hard about appraising ideas or situations? What is easy?*

Learning Outcome

Use the learning outcome to frame the purpose and relevance of Listening 1. Ask: *What did you learn from Listening 1 that prepares you to participate in a group discussion on how to encourage children to exhibit good sportsmanship?* (Students learned how children become athletes in China. They may want to use these ideas in the group discussion.)

Listening Skill: Listening for causes and effects (20 minutes)

)) CD4, Track 15

1. Present the information on cause and effect and play the audio when prompted.

2. Check comprehension. Ask: *What are some signal words speakers use to show cause? What are some signal words speakers use to show effect? How is this information helpful for you as an English language learner?*

▶ *Listening and Speaking 4, page 205*

A (5 minutes)

 CD4, Track 16

1. Direct students to preview the choices for each item.

2. Play the audio as students select their answers.

3. Check the answers as a class.

> **Activity A Answers, p. 205**
> **1.** a;   **2.** b;   **3.** b;   **4.** b;   **5.** a;   **6.** a

B (10 minutes)

1. Read the directions aloud. Have students complete the activity individually.

2. Check the answers as a class. Ask students to support their answers by pointing out the signal words in the sentences.

> **Activity B Answers, p. 205**
> **1.** E;   **2.** C;   **3.** E;   **4.** E;   **5.** C;   **6.** C

 For additional practice with listening for causes and effects, have students visit *Q Online Practice*.

Tip for Success (1 minute)

1. Ask a volunteer to read the tip aloud.

2. Remind students that a conscious focus on discerning causes and effects now will help them make these distinctions more naturally later.

▶ *Listening and Speaking 4, page 206*

LISTENING 2: *Until It Hurts* Discusses Youth Sports Obsession

VOCABULARY (20 minutes)

1. Write the vocabulary words on the board and model pronunciation. Ask: *What words do you already know? What do those words mean?*

2. Put students in groups and have them complete the activity. Answer any questions about meaning and provide examples of the words in context.

3. Call on volunteers to read the sentences aloud.

4. If time allows, ask volunteers to create new sentences with the vocabulary.

> **Vocabulary Answers, pp. 206–207**
> **1.** journalist;   **2.** obsession;   **3.** fundamental;
> **4.** vulnerable;   **5.** burnout;   **6.** former;
> **7.** ambition;   **8.** ultimately;   **9.** spectator;
> **10.** reasonable;   **11.** regret;   **12.** escalate

 For additional practice with the vocabulary, have students visit *Q Online Practice*.

▶ *Listening and Speaking 4, page 207*

PREVIEW LISTENING 2 (5 minutes)

1. Read the introduction aloud. Direct students to discuss the question with a partner.

2. Tell students they should review their answers after the listening.

> **Preview Listening 2 Answer, p. 207**
> Answers will vary.

Listening 2 Background Note

Mark Hyman is a sports journalist, a former athlete, and a public speaker. Based out of Baltimore, Maryland, in the United States, Hyman also teaches at the college level and sometimes coaches baseball.

LISTEN FOR MAIN IDEAS

 CD4, Track 17

A (15 minutes)

1. Read the directions and preview the chart with students. Have students copy the chart into their notebooks.

2. Play the audio as students complete the chart individually.

3. Elicit answers from volunteers.

> **Activity A Answers, p. 207**
> Answers may vary. Possible answers:
> Major changes in youth sports:
> **1.** Children start at a very young age.
> **2.** Child athletes commonly specialize in one particular sport.
> Negative effects of these changes:
> **1.** Overuse injuries
> **2.** Burnout

B (10 minutes)

1. Have students answer the questions and discuss their answers in pairs.

2. Call on volunteers to share their answers with the class.

> **Activity B Answers, p. 207**
> Answers may vary. Possible answers:
> 1. Now: Sports are run by parents.
>   Then (150 years ago): Sports were done to teach skills, have fun, and build character.
> 2. Listen to doctors to avoid overuse injuries; Discourage kids from playing only one sport year round; Listen to kids and help them decide how and when to play; Encourage parents to be reasonable.

 Listening and Speaking 4, page 208

LISTEN FOR DETAILS (10 minutes)

 CD4, Track 18

1. Direct students to read the statements and possible answers before they listen again.

2. Play the audio as students circle their answers.

3. Have students compare answers with a partner. Replay the audio if necessary.

4. Go over the answers with the class.

> **Listen for Details Answers, p. 208**
> **1.** b; **2.** c; **3.** a; **4.** b; **5.** b; **6.** a

For additional practice with listening comprehension, have students visit *Q Online Practice*.

Listening and Speaking 4, page 209

WHAT DO YOU THINK?

A (15 minutes)

1. Ask students to read the questions and reflect on their answers.

2. Seat students in small groups and assign roles: a group leader to make sure everyone contributes, a note-taker to record the group's ideas, a reporter to share the group's ideas with the class, and a timekeeper to watch the clock.

3. Give students ten minutes to discuss the questions. Call time if conversations are winding down. Allow extra time if necessary.

4. Call on each group's reporter to share ideas with the class.

> **Activity A Answers, p. 209**
> Answers will vary. Possible answers:
> 1. Parents get their children involved in competitive sports because they want their children to understand the importance of trying to reach a goal even if you don't end up being number one. There is competition everywhere—in school, on the playground, in the workplace—so I think it's OK for parents to expose their children to a little competition as long as no one takes things too seriously.
> 2. Parents and coaches should emphasize building character and having fun over winning. If they avoid pushing children, then kids will not burn out or injure themselves.

B (10 minutes)

1. Have students continue working in their small groups to discuss the questions in Activity B. Tell them to choose a new leader, note-taker, reporter, and timekeeper.

2. Call on the new reporter to share the group's answers to the questions.

> **Activity B Answers, p. 209**
> Answers will vary. Possible answers:
> 1. Young Chinese and American athletes are learning how to set and meet extremely difficult goals. They also are learning how to deal with failure as well as handle success.
> 2. In special schools in China and youth sports leagues, young athletes have to deal with the pressure of being successful at a level that most people cannot achieve. At the same time, they must try to have a normal childhood.

Learning Outcome

Use the learning outcome to frame the purpose and relevance of Listenings 1 and 2. Ask: *What did you learn that prepares you to participate in a group discussion about how to encourage children to exhibit good sportsmanship?* (Students learned about the pressures and problems child athletes face. These ideas may help them in their group discussion.)

Vocabulary Skill: Idioms (10 minutes)

1. Ask: *Do you know what an idiom is? What idioms have you heard before?* List them on the board.

2. Present the information on idioms. Ask students to read the examples.

3. Check comprehension: *What's an idiom? What does* make a point of *mean? How many idioms are there? How can you figure out the meaning of idioms?*

Skill Note

People often use idioms when speaking. Idioms are difficult for language learners because their meanings are not literal. Therefore, students need to be exposed to idioms so that they can understand a speaker when idioms are used in conversation.

EXPANSION ACTIVITY: Idiom Pictures (20 minutes)

1. Put students into pairs or small groups and give them a sentence that contains an idiom. Make sure to choose idioms that students will be able to visualize. You may want to choose idioms from this unit or others, such as *a big fish in a small pond, a shot in the dark, a fly on the wall, etc.*

2. Ask the pairs/groups to read their sentence and try to determine what the idiom means. Provide assistance as necessary.

3. Then have students draw a picture that represents the idiom and write a new sentence below the picture, using the idiom.

4. Ask groups to present their pictures and teach their idioms to the rest of the class.

Tip for Success (1 minute)

1. Have students read the tip silently.

2. Ask students: *What kinds of clarification questions can you ask when you don't understand what someone has said?*

▶ *Listening and Speaking 4, page 210*

A (10 minutes)

CD4, Track 19

1. Read the directions aloud.

2. Play the audio and have students select their answers. Then ask students to share their answers with a partner.

3. Check the answers as a class.

> **Activity A Answers, p. 210**
> **1.** e; **2.** b; **3.** d; **4.** a; **5.** c

B (15 minutes)

1. Direct students to complete the activity. Circulate around the room and provide support as needed.

2. When the students have finished writing, ask them to read their sentences to a partner.

3. Choose a few volunteers to write sentences on the board. Elicit corrections as needed.

4. Then have students practice saying the sentences.

Activity B Answers, p. 210
Answers will vary.

> **MULTILEVEL OPTION**
>
> Have lower-level students work in pairs to write the sentences with idioms.

Tip for Success (3 minutes)

1. Read the tip aloud.

2. Ask students to look in their dictionaries for information about collocation patterns. Remind students that, often, words naturally go together in English. The more chunks a person knows, the more natural his or her speech can be.

▶ *Listening and Speaking 4, page 211*

SPEAKING

Grammar: Use of real conditionals
(20 minutes)

CD4, Track 20

1. Present the information on real conditionals and play the audio when prompted. Elicit and answer questions from students as they arise.

2. Check comprehension by asking questions: *What is a real conditional? What types of clauses are a part of a real conditional construction? What kinds of ideas are expressed by the real conditional?*

Skill Note

Conditional sentences express the dependence of one set of circumstances on another. When an *if* clause occurs first, the word *then* may be used before the main clause. For example, *If Brazil's team wins tonight, then they will be in first place.* Note that *then* cannot be used in this way if the conditional clause begins with *when*. Also, the use of the modals *should, may,* and *might* in a main clause makes the future outcome less certain than when *will* or *going to* are used. For example, *If we arrive early, we'll find a good parking spot* vs. *If we arrive early, we may find a good parking spot.*

▶ *Listening and Speaking 4, page 212*

A (15 minutes)

1. Read the directions and complete the first sentence as an example.

2. Have students work individually to write their sentences. Then have them compare their sentences with a partner.

3. Call on volunteers to write their sentences on the board. Elicit corrections as needed.

Activity A Answers, p. 212
1. When the rain stops, we can continue the game.
2. If you want to go to the game, I can give you my tickets.
3. If you're too sick to go to practice, you should stay home.
4. When I have a headache, I don't like the noise of cheering.
5. When we get to the baseball field, I'll put on my uniform.
6. If the game is canceled, we'll play again next week.
7. If you don't show up to the team meeting, you can't play.
8. If you miss this shot, my team wins.

B (15 minutes)

1. Read the directions as a class.

2. Ask students to complete the activity individually.

3. Ask volunteers to write their sentences on the board. Elicit any alternate sentences from other students.

Activity B Answers, pp. 212–213
Answers will vary slightly. Possible answers:
1. If she misses the next practice session, I am going to suspend her from the team.
2. I can drive you to the game if you buy gas for my car.
3. If we win the next game, we will win a prize.
4. If you hold the bat correctly, you might be able to hit the baseball.

 For additional practice with real conditionals, have students visit *Q Online Practice*.

 Listening and Speaking 4, page 213

Pronunciation: Thought groups
(15 minutes)

 CD4, Track 21

1. Present the information on thought groups. Play the audio and ask students to repeat the examples. Make sure students exaggerate the pauses between thought groups.

2. Check comprehension. Ask: *What's a thought group? Why do speakers use them?*

3. Write a new sentence on the board and ask the students to separate it into thought groups (e.g., I was walking / to the store / the other day / when I saw / my old friend Bert.).

A (10 minutes)
CD4, Track 22

1. Direct students to preview the sentences and think about where the thought groups might fall.

2. Play the audio and have students mark the thought groups. Put students in pairs to compare answers.

3. Elicit answers from volunteers.

Activity A Answers, pp. 213–214
1. In my opinion, / that's a bad idea.
2. Are they coming, / or not?
3. If I get home early / I'll go running. / Want to join me?
4. Keep your head up / as you kick the ball. / It's important.
5. All week long / these kids are so busy / they have no time for fun.
6. If she wins this match, / Ms. Williams will be in first place.
7. If you'd like to talk, / call me at / (555) / 233 - / 1157.
8. Here's my e-mail address: / goalkeeper100 / @ / global / .us.

▶ *Listening and Speaking 4, page 214*

B (10 minutes)

1. Pair students and ask them to read the sentences in Activity A, pausing between thought groups. Circulate around the room and offer feedback.

2. Ask a few volunteers to read sentences for the class. Highlight their use of thought groups.

For additional practice with thought groups, have students visit *Q Online Practice*.

21ST CENTURY SKILLS

Collaboration, and not competition, is what produces cohesion in the workplace and classroom. When you work every day with the same people, everyone has to get along most of the time. Therefore, anything people can do to encourage and sustain collaboration goes a long way toward creating positive workplace energy. The following skill, adding to another speaker's comments, is one way to practice collaboration.

Speaking Skill: Adding to another speaker's comments (10 minutes)

🔊 CD4, Track 23

1. Ask volunteers to read the text aloud. Provide further explanation or examples as needed. Play the audio when prompted.

2. Check comprehension: *Why is it a good idea to build on someone else's ideas? What phrases can build on an idea? What phrases can show agreement?*

▶ *Listening and Speaking 4, page 215*

A (10 minutes)

🔊 CD4, Track 24

1. Have a volunteer read the directions aloud.

2. Play the audio as students select their answers.

3. Put students into pairs to compare answers. Check answers as a class.

> **Activity A Answers, p. 215**
> Checked: Another important point is that…; And to build on what John said earlier, …; And I would add that …;That's a good point.

B (10 minutes)

1. Ask students to work individually to complete the activity.

2. Elicit ideas from the class and list them on the board.

> **Activity B Answers, p. 215**
> Answers will vary.

C (10 minutes)

1. Place students into groups and have them share their answers for Activity B. Remind students to add on to each other's comments using the language they've just learned.

2. Circulate around the room to ensure that students are adding on to others' comments.

 For additional practice with adding to another speaker's comments, have students visit *Q Online Practice.*

Unit Assignment: Share opinions about sportsmanship

Unit Question (5 minutes)

Refer students back to the ideas they discussed at the beginning of the unit about whether athletic competition is good for children. Cue students if necessary by asking specific questions about the content of the unit: *Does competition help or hurt children? In what ways does it help them? How might it not be good for them?* Read the direction lines for the assignment together to ensure understanding.

Learning Outcome

1. Tie the Unit Assignment to the unit learning outcome. Say: *The outcome for this unit is to participate in a group discussion about how to encourage children to exhibit good sportsmanship. The Unit Assignment is going to let you show your skills in speaking in a group discussion, using real conditionals, adding to others' comments, and speaking in thought groups.*

2. Explain that you are going to use a rubric similar to their Self-Assessment checklist on p. 218 to grade their Unit Assignment. Share with students a copy of the rubric on p. 108 of this *Teacher's Handbook* so they have a specific understanding of how they will be assessed.

▶ *Listening and Speaking 4, page 216*

Consider the Ideas (15 minutes)

1. Ask a volunteer to read the questions aloud.

2. Put students into pairs and have them discuss the questions. Encourage them to take notes on their answers.

3. Elicit answers and reasons from volunteers.

Prepare and Speak

Gather Ideas

A (15 minutes)

1. Read the directions together.

2. Have students form groups to brainstorm ideas together and take notes.

Tip for Success (5 minutes)

1. Read the Tip for Success.

2. Ask students how they use note-taking in their classes. Point out that note-takers retain information longer than those who don't take notes.

Organize Ideas

B (10 minutes)

1. Based upon their results in Activity A, ask students to expand upon the group's best ideas and fill out the chart.

2. Circulate around the room and make sure the benefits to children make sense in relation to the ways to get involved and encourage sportsmanship.

▶ *Listening and Speaking 4, page 218*

Speak

C (20 minutes)

1. Review the directions with the class. With their same group, have students discuss the topic: how and why should we encourage good sportsmanship in children.

2. Use the Unit Assignment Rubric on p. 108 of this *Teacher's Handbook* to score each student's presentation.

3. Alternatively, have one group conduct their discussion for another group. Have listeners complete the Unit Assignment Rubric for those in the discussion.

Alternative Unit Assignments

Assign or have students choose one of these assignments to do instead of, or in addition to, the Unit Assignment.

1. Think about ways, other than sports, in which you competed with others when you were a child. For instance, did you compete academically or with siblings at home? Was the experience negative, positive, or both? Explain the experience to your classmates.

2. Research a child athlete or an adult athlete who achieved stardom at a young age (e.g., Rafael Nadal, Lebron James, Michelle Wie). Present a report to the class in which you describe some of the challenges and successes the young athlete experienced.

 For an additional Unit Assignment, have students visit *Q Online Practice.*

Check and Reflect

Check

A (10 minutes)

1. Direct students to read and complete the Self-Assessment checklist.

2. Ask for a show of hands for how many students gave all or mostly *yes* answers. Congratulate them on their success.

3. Remind students that they can always refer to the checklist before they begin the Unit Assignment so they can focus on the skills they need to complete the assignment successfully.

Reflect

B (10 minutes)

Ask students to consider the questions in pairs. When the conversations have died down, have students share something new they have learned. Ask: *How did your ideas about competitive sports change as we worked through this unit?*

▶ *Listening and Speaking 4, page 219*

Track Your Success (5 minutes)

1. Have students circle the words they have learned in this unit. Suggest that students go back through the unit to review any words they have forgotten.

2. Have students check the skills they have mastered. If students need more practice to feel confident about their proficiency in a skill, point out the page numbers and encourage them to review.

3. Read the learning outcome aloud (*Participate in a group discussion, sharing opinions on how to encourage children to exhibit good sportsmanship*). Ask students if they feel that they have met the outcome.

Unit 10   Child's Play

Unit Assignment Rubric

Student name: _____

Date: _____

Unit Assignment: *Share opinions about sportsmanship.*

20 points = Discussion element was completely successful (at least 90% of the time).
15 points = Discussion element was mostly successful (at least 70% of the time).
10 points = Discussion element was partially successful (at least 50% of the time).
 0 points = Discussion element was not successful.

Share Opinions	20 points	15 points	10 points	0 points
Student clearly explained how to encourage good sportsmanship and why this is important.				
Student used real conditional sentences correctly.				
Student used vocabulary from the unit.				
Student added to another speaker's comments.				
Student spoke in thought groups.				

Total points: _____

Comments:

Welcome to the Q Testing Program

1. MINIMUM SYSTEM REQUIREMENTS[1]

1024 x 768 screen resolution displaying 32-bit color

Web browser[2]:
Windows®-requires Internet Explorer® 7 or above
Mac®-requires OS X v10.4 and Safari® 2.0 or above
Linux®-requires Mozilla® 1.7 or Firefox® 1.5.0.9 or above

To open and use the customizable tests you must have an application installed that will open and edit .doc files, such as Microsoft® Word® (97 or higher).

To view and print the Print-and-go Tests, you must have an application installed that will open and print .pdf files, such as Adobe® Acrobat® Reader (6.0 or higher).

2. RUNNING THE APPLICATION

Windows®/Mac®
- Ensure that no other applications are running.
- Insert the Q: Skills for Success Testing Program CD-ROM into your CD-ROM drive.
- Double click on the file "start.htm" to start.

Linux®
- Insert the Q: Skills for Success Testing Program CD-ROM into your CD-ROM drive.
- Mount the disk on to the desktop.
- Double click on the CD-ROM icon.
- Right click on the icon for the "start.htm" file and select to "open with Mozilla".

3. TECHNICAL SUPPORT

If you experience any problems with this CD-ROM, please check that your machine matches or exceeds the minimum system requirements in point 1 above and that you are following the steps outlined in point 2 above.

If this does not help, e-mail us with your query at: elt.cdsupport.uk@oup.com
Be sure to provide the following information:

- Operating system (e.g. Windows 2000, Service Pack 4)
- Application used to access content, and version number
- Amount of RAM
- Processor speed
- Description of error or problem
- Actions before error occurred
- Number of times the error has occurred
- Is the error repeatable?

---

[1] The Q Testing Program CD-ROM also plays its audio files in a conventional CD player.

[2] Note that when browsing the CD-ROM in your Web browser, you must have pop-up windows enabled in your Web browser settings.

The Q Testing Program

The disc on the inside back cover of this book contains both ready-made and customizable versions of **Reading and Writing** and **Listening and Speaking** tests. Each of the tests consists of multiple choice, fill-in-the-blanks/sentence completion, error correction, sentence reordering/sentence construction, and matching exercises.

Creating and Using Tests

1. Select "Reading and Writing Tests" or "Listening and Speaking Tests" from the main menu.

2. Select the appropriate unit test or cumulative test (placement, midterm, or final) from the left-hand column.

3. For ready-made tests, select a Print-and-go Test, Answer Key, and Audio Script (for Listening and Speaking tests).

4. To modify tests for your students, select a Customizable Test, Answer Key, and Audio Script (for Listening and Speaking tests). Save the file to your computer and edit the test using Microsoft Word or a compatible word processor.

5. For Listening and Speaking tests, use the audio tracks provided with the tests. **Audio files for the listening and speaking tests can also be played in a standard CD player.**

Reading and Writing Tests

Each test consists of 40 questions taken from the selected unit. The Reading and Writing Tests assess reading skills, vocabulary, vocabulary skills, grammar, and writing skills.

Listening and Speaking Tests

Each test consists of 40 questions taken from the selected unit. The Listening and Speaking Tests assess listening skills, vocabulary, vocabulary skills, grammar, pronunciation, and speaking skills.

Cumulative Tests

The placement tests for both Listening and Speaking and Reading and Writing consist of 50 questions. Each placement test places students in the correct level of Q: Introductory–5. **A printable User Guide to help you administer the placement test is included with the placement test files on the CD-ROM.**

The midterm tests for both Listening and Speaking and Reading and Writing consist of 25 questions covering Units 1–5 of the selected Level. The midterm Reading and Listening texts are new and not used in any other tests or student books.

The final tests for both Listening and Speaking and Reading and Writing consist of 25 questions covering Units 6–10 of the selected Level. The final Reading and Listening texts are new and not used in any other tests or student books.